Sacred Fire of Twin-flames

By

Katrina Bowlin-MacKenzie

Cover

By

Phoenix MacKenzie

Published by Katrina Bowlin-MacKenzie

First printing May 2013

ISBN-13: 978-1489560353
ISBN-10: 1489560351

All information in this book is the opinion of the author and the contributors, if it does not resonate with you, then you need to find your own, by research and meditation.

To contact the author send your emails to:
myst.weaver@yahoo.com

Dedication

I wish to thank my beloved husband and Twin-flame Phoenix for his cover image and all his contributions to this book.

I would like to thank all the Twin-flame couples that bared their souls to tell their personal stories.

And I would like to thank my wonderful proofreaders, Marcia and Malika, who are always there for me.

THE OCEAN

Storm driven by impassioned moon

she is the ocean

across tides of time

calling to her souls groom

"where" the wind whispers

"where is love, where?"

Her life cold grey skies

of beaten crushing sadness

rains and veils of fog

the tears of her despair

Her grace cut upon rocks

lifeless hearts of man's brutality

Ever she heals

ever she gives of her life

Upon a shore her soul drifted

to merge with sacred rivers of compassion

in harbors of peace

and into her waters love flows

Her waves lap against my brow

Her passion ebbs and flows

to my beating heart

as sea and shore roll the surf

and each lap whispers love

So blue and clear the ocean now

mirror of heaven and eternal skies

So deep I swim within her embrace

I, I the suns child and spirit

reaching with light

to her depths that have known

no warmth from this world

Be still my love, my ocean

carry my light, my love

Flow through me now

let my fire open thy heart

and we shall become the myst

tears of God in loves joy.

©Phoenix MacKenzie

Table of contents

Chapter One

Definitions

1. Soul Families

Your Soul family is the family your soul belongs to. These are people you reincarnate with over and over. They are seeking the same soul advancement as you. They are usually your physical family, friends, lovers etc.

2. Soul Fragments

A soul fragment is a part of your soul. Souls split into fragments and each fragment then goes into different lives to advance your soul. Soul fragments often live parallel lives as one another.

3. Parallel lives

A parallel live is another life a fragment of your soul is living at the same time as you. It may be hard to understand, but past, present and future lives are all lived as parallel lives, that are happening at the same time. Time is not as we perceive it on earth. There is no such thing as time as all things are happening simultaneously.

4.   Soul-mates

A Soul-mate is most often one of your soul family. It is a soul that vibrates on the same level as your own soul. Soul-mates can be siblings, parents, lovers and you have experienced all of that with Soul-mates.

5.   Walk-ins

A Walk-in takes place when the soul in the body is finished or no longer wants to remain in the body. An agreement is made between the higher selves of these two souls and an exchange is made. Usually the soul leaving the body is experiencing suicidal tendencies and the exchange is usually made during an illness or an accident. One soul leaves and the other enters the body. There is an adjustment period where the new soul gets used to the exchange. Often the incoming soul, since they have forgotten the agreement upon arrival, are confused and do not know what is happening as they are suddenly in a body they don't recognize and have no idea who they or people around them are.

6.   Soul Braiding

Is a Walk-in experience but neither soul leaves the body and they share it. Sort of like a possession.

7.   Twin-flames

Your Twin-flame is the other half of your
soul. Many years ago Souls divided into two
parts or fragments, a negative and a positive,
masculine and feminine. From that point on
these souls have been seeking their other
half.

While you spend many lifetimes with your
Twin, it is usually in a Soul-mate capacity,
rarely do you find them in a lover
relationship. Recently with the arrival of the
new age and energy more and more Twin-
flames are finding each other. The reason
for this is that it is a time of spiritual
advancement, enlightenment of the Human
Race and what better way to teach spiritual
enlightenment than to reunite Twin-flames to
teach the world that love is the only thing
there is?

By Katrina

Twin Flames, Soul Family and Soul Mates.

Firstly let's get a grasp on what a soul is. I'm sure you've heard of terms like: 'As above - so below' Yin and Yang, 'Made in God's image' or perhaps Microcosm (small) and Macrocosm (large). These all refer to polarities, duality or reflections. What nature shows us on this world can be related to the wider multiverse including none physical realms, which some may call 'spiritual realms'.

All things in the physical realm have an atomic structure; atoms are made of smaller things like neutrons, protons, electrons and so on. Let's bunch them all up and call them 'particles'. Taking the principle of 'as above - so below', the 'spiritual', metaphysical realms have their version of particles. All particles are stimulated to vibrate by spirit, which you could perceive as the hum of creation or God's great gong if you like. Scientists might like to think of it as 'the big bang'. It is the frequency at which particles vibrate which defines their form, and the collective orchestras are termed as glass, wood, thought, moonbeams or whatever.

What? No Amy, I said: gong, God's great...

Oh never mind.

An example of how the metaphysical realms mirror the physical realm in some respects is that our physical body has a psychic duplicate. We have physical and metaphysical lungs, heart, legs, eyes etc. So while the 'spiritual' realm may not have cars and hot dogs or even atoms, it has its energies, some of which reflect aspects of our physical dimension. Another example is that some mediums can see those who have passed over in human form. Ghosts might be another example.

In a sense soul is a particle of God/dess, ah but isn't everything a particle of God/dess you pantheists may ask. Indeed, but just as we are made up of different particles, we are physical, emotional, and astral, we have consciousness, thought etc, then God/dess, in its own unfathomable way also has different facets. Soul would be like a sense, as some say: 'God exploring itself'. Souls are like probes gathering information about creation. Our mind senses the body's internal goings on because something informs it. That 'something' in divine terms is soul.

While there are various perspectives of God/dess, if we set aside the fine print and focus on fundamental concepts: God/dess is the creative force or entity. So whether you say God/dess created us ('in his own image') or God/dess is us, we all come from that source. Each of us exists in different dimensions or 'frequencies' simultaneously: physical, astral, emotional, mental, soul, soul consciousness etc. Little 'we' (microcosm) mirror the multiverse (macrocosm) that has many dimensions. Some, like our beings, are denser frequencies than others: ranging from soul to physical. Soul itself is the purest frequency and thus closest to the 'source' of all frequency: God/dess. We are the beat pumping out of the Almighty's radio show as it were.

No Tom I have no idea where God purchased his bass booster from or whether that what caused the big bang.

From source souls issue forth, one way or another they are 'of God/dess'. This we might compare to an egg leaving an ovary and entering the womb: chalice of life or cradle of existence. What we have at this point is LIFE, when that first spark of life encounters polarity: LOVE (feminine) and LIGHT (masculine) what happens? HEY, hey no giggling at the back there! Yes our little egg gets fertilized and splits into two cells. Gradually it grows into something that makes lots of noise and stinks, but that's getting a bit ahead of ourselves.

Erm... Oh yes, so in regard to souls, the influence of polarity is the first layer of a souls consciousness (soul personality, higher self etc). Somewhat like an electro magnet, charged by polarity, (duality), the soul attracts cause and effect: simple vibrational experience, which leads to its consciousness being different from others. Its experiences are unique and therefore IT becomes unique: a character, a personality in a very simplistic way, and that is why soul personality (higher self), is NOT the soul, it is a persona. When we say soul mates, it is not the soul itself; it is the persona, the souls consciousness that we are referring to. All souls are identical, they never change, it is the consciousness that changes. That consciousness is often referred to as 'The Inner Master', 'The Self', when it is said: "Know Thy Self" it is the higher self, the master within, your immortal self that is being referred to.

So we have a trinity: Soul, higher self, physical self and we have a trinity: Love, Light and Life. Do you see a pattern forming? Dimension one = soul, dimension two = duality, polarity (Love and Light), dimension three = hot dogs etc. And I'll throw in a few more mystical freebees: 3x3 is

16

the number of Mastery (9) after which we return to 0, zero, infinity, God/dess or what some term as 'Christ consciousness'. It all makes a lot of sense when you see how the numbers, physics and metaphysics all flow together in harmony. It is in the perception and understanding of this grand architecture that we come 'closer to God' not through blind faith in 'maybes'.

Right, so back to our soul and physical comparison: egg. Egg gets fertilized cells split; soul encounters polarity (Love and Light). The soul splits in a sense, one predominantly masculine, and one feminine. This is what we call TWIN FLAMES: two halves of the prime, Adam and Eve if you like. When Love and Light are in perfect harmony they create a spark (Life). This principle is known as the law of the triangle or law of manifestation. So another soul issues forth and divides and we again have twin flames: in a sense child of the first twins Adam and Eve. Now we begin to have SOUL FAMILY. There's Life sparks going off all over the place, Love and Light are at it like rabbits, we got Brothers and Sisters squabbling over who gets what star and so forth.

Yes, you there in the second row with your hand up... Incest? Well yes in a way, but then how many people started the human race? Yep, sorry your Mommy and Daddy are more than likely distant relatives. On a soul level we call this SOUL MATES. Over eons of time soul consciousness grows through life experience, a personality, individual resonance becomes ever more distinct. Soul personalities that have a similar level and type of experience through dimensions, such as this third one, will resonate a similar frequency; they may be drawn to each other in many incarnations and share experiences. This is why soul mates are often mistaken for twin flames: we dig each other's vibes. Question is should you really have a relationship with your best friend? I mean as friends you're great but... *Sigh*

After a few weeks... Okay billions of years, soul personality (higher consciousness) evolves, as does the physical projection it designs, you know, like human beamings and such. These designs are formed from countless experiences, the sum total of all we have been, such as insects, fish, birds, reptiles, wolves, snakes, zods from planet Zit and other incarnations. We evolve spiritually, metaphysically as we evolve physically. Higher consciousness demands more and more complex or refined forms through which it gains experience, awareness.

Beyond this world other races or species have evolved, many of which moved on from this 'dense' third dimensional universe. As their forms become ever more 'refined', subtle, of a purer, higher frequency, there are fewer barriers to consciousness. In short their minds become one, while still individual parts of a whole they gradually become a single entity; a species becomes a 'body'. Just as souls are particles of God/dess, beings become particles or cells of a body an entire species. These we might also term as 'SOUL FAMILY', angels are an example you are all familiar with, the Phoeni is another good example: there is only ever one Phoenix, yet it is of many flames.

THE BARRIERS AND OVERCOMING THEM

You would think that being twin flames is enough for two people to be together, to live in love and harmony. Unfortunately this is rarely the case. Twin flames are usually separated by their differences and cannot be truly united until those differences, that time and experiences have created, are 'worked out'. I mean that quite literally and refer to 'spiritual work'. Bear in mind that you are twins on the deepest level, this resonates out to your physical self. However, the further from source, the greater the impurities. The inner flame must be brought forth, to be a beacon for your twin to find you in this dense physical realm. That's not to say you must both be perfect.

The fundamental key to this work, the key to Life, duality, harmony, manifestation, everything is: BALANCE.

Unfortunately in this 'new age' era there are many misleading concepts, which do not conform to this fundamental principle. For example the idea that heart is true and mind lies is utter 'Lala'. It would be like saying women are true and men are lies or Love is right and Light is wrong. While society as a whole needs to focus more on the heart, to attain balance, both heart and mind must harmonize. They act as each other's guide and guardians, together they attain truth, one without the other is a flame divided. So be careful what you 'believe', always apply the principle of balance to your work.

As with a planet's atmosphere, or indeed the multiverse, we have many layers, our microcosmic selves mirror this macrocosmic principle: our aura and Etheric bodies, our karma, mind, emotions and so on. Those of us in the spiritual community know the importance of aligning and purifying chakras, cleansing the aura, and in time honored traditions of spiritual alchemy: attaining a golden aura (purity). All of this work is focused on refining, attuning the physical, mental, and emotional, Etheric self with the inner self. It is that inner self which is the flame, if our outer self doesn't resonate the inner then we cannot resonate with our twin.

Over countless incarnations karma, oaths, vows and other baggage stacks up. For twins to be united this has to be cleansed, each must be pure, naked metaphorically speaking. No sorry Lucy I don't know of any metaphorical showers. So before meeting Mr. or Missy Right we need to get our house in order. Fluff those pillows girls and guys pick up those socks... Erm, in fact just trash them guys, yeah they're seriously rank... Metaphorically speaking. Though in all seriousness I should say that some concepts of what a man should be and what a woman should be need to go out the archaic window as well. Yep fraid so Tarzan.

There are various methods of releasing baggage, not only oaths, but also emotional and psychological bonds with other people from your past. I'll just suggest two of them:

Cycles End.

Requirements:

One full moon and one black candle.

A few minutes before midnight on a full moon, light your black candle. Both the full moon and midnight are the end of cycles. Black attracts and absorbs vibrations, the flame purifies them. Spend a few minutes releasing what you wish to the flame, finally state the following:

"Sacred fire, to thee I relinquish all and any vows, oaths, promises I have made before this day. No longer am I bound to them. So be it."

Know that all vows and oaths made in this and any other incarnation are being consumes by the flame, like old scrolls burning in a fire, gone forever. At midnight extinguish the candle. (Don't blow it out, us a snuffer or wet fingertips.)

Rebirth

Each day select a person from your memories who has hurt you, been a negative influence in your life - the alcoholic father, the manager that ruined your career, the spouse that cheated, the Doctor's mistakes, the Brother that wasn't there for you, the hamster that ate your Birthday cake... Whatever and whoever it is.

Now you are going to heal that moment, your connection with that person. First of all you should select a candle that's color intuitively feels right for healing this memory.

Violet = Love in the unconditional sense.
Light blue = Healing
Green = Earthly connections, emotions etc
Yellow = Thought processes, stress, ego

Having lit a candle, close your eyes and visualize the person standing by a river, try not to focus on a negative memory of them, just see the person standing before you in an non-threatening way that involves no power struggles etc. This is a peaceful place by a shallow river, its waters moving swiftly swirling around small rocks and washing over pebbles. There is a path that leads away into some woods beyond which is a bright meadow sloping down a hillside at the bottom of which mist gently hovers.

Say to this person (for example):

"Whatever has past has past, In Love I embrace you, and in Love I free you. I am going now, before I do I want you to know that I hold no grievances, what is done is done. I hope you will accept my love and that it will help you along your path, my own path leads another way. Farewell and may life offer many blessings for you."

Hug them or shake their hand, whatever feels right as a gesture of love and feel love for them. Rise above what happened, heal the moment, transform that circumstance and see a shroud of violet light about them. As a parting gesture smile, wish them well, Watch as they begin to walk away into the wood. There is a chord that flows from you to them, like an Etheric telephone wire, take a knife, sword or scissors and cut that chord now. It falls away and you can see that person gradually fading from your vision. They no longer exist as part of your reality or part of your being.

You might feel a shift in energies, light headed afterwards, this is because you have been carrying a huge weight around, probably for years, and it's gone now. One by one, day by day heal another, release another chain (chord). This ceremony is also important in existing relationships and for those acting as a caregiver for other people. You may not actually want to let go of that person, but what you should do is release the exchange of energy draining that may be occurring. Cutting the chord allows you to establish a more positive connection with them.

(Part two)

You are alone now, amidst the beauty of nature, standing at the rivers edge, the river is shallow, and you see water flowing swiftly over rocks and pebbles. Remove your clothes, there is no one around, but if that makes you feel uncomfortable just stand bare footed and then walk into the river. Acknowledge the fact that you are human, at least in the incarnate state, and that we ALL make mistakes. That was the old you though, its done, past and must not prevent you from being what you want to be.

In the water you see a reflection of yourself, through that reflection, as if it were speaking to you, say:

"I forgive you because I love you (your name), I love what you are becoming. It is a wonder, it is beautiful, I love you for this moment that at long last 'we' share. It's good to be back."

Now think of some moment, a memory of guilt or shame. Imagine it as being like a small brown or heavy energy cloud that you are too light now (in every sense of the word light) to hold any-more. Gravity is pushing it down through you, into your feet, still it cannot hold and the water carries it away, you see it dispersing and flowing away with the river knowing that energy will soon be purified by minerals and crystals in the river, it will never exist again. If you find that it won't go away, again imagine there is a chord connecting you to it and cut that chord - whoosh its gone. Now say to your reflection:

"You are healed, healthy, happy, loved, I appreciate you so much."

Hold out your arms to the reflection, see it rise from the water like a translucent you and feel it merging with you until in peace you are no longer 'we', you are 'I'. There is a waterfall nearby, stand within it and allow its cleansing waters to cascade through your being and wash all your connections to the past away.

Now walk to the other side of the river where a white cloak has been waiting for you; resting in the grass. As you put it on it feels so incredible soft and warm, it is a gift to yourself because you're worth it. As you relax there say:

"I am perfect as I AM"

To complete the ceremony, extinguish your candle, do not blow it out, and peacefully snuff the flame. What was is now extinguished.

Notes:

There are some people and events in our lives that are very difficult to release, to think of that person with love may seem impossible. However, I would ask you to contemplate that each event is a lesson in life, that persons soul may have entered into a spiritual contract with your own as YOUR soul deemed the experience necessary. The other person will endure the karma of what they have done for YOUR benefit, no matter how painful the experience.

Maybe their only savour in this is for you to help them heal the karma that they endure for your sake. Indeed then it is not only a matter of forgiveness but also one of compassion, gratitude and Love. If you can learn to release them with love and embrace this understanding you will have achieved a great deal on your path, opening yourself to higher energies, which will manifest in your life, you may well be surprised at just how much.

--*--

Goes without saying that your twin is someone very special, you wouldn't want to judge them by the habits of other people that you've shared your life with, or carry the way you have been mistreated into the twin relationship. Whether you're going to save the world together or just be happy bunnies in a snugly hole, the cleansing aspect of spiritual work is very important.

The frequently bad ending with soul mates, who help to prepare you for meeting your twin, may well be to adjust personality traits. Little sensitive Miss Pisces meets a roaring Leo twin. Yep well you're both equals Mr. Leo! What was that Miss Pisces? Yes you to, you tell him to pick his own damn socks up. Yes folks it's stereotyping time! But you get the gist. For example I'm a bull, chillin in my field, Katrina has a lot of lioness in her. A soul mate taught me to snort a lot rather than doing the Taurus thing of reaching a point where I see red and enter the proverbial china shop.

It may seem incomprehensible that as you spent countless incarnations as a buwadder from the Serrealian Domain while your twin spent as long as a gin binger from the Trypdingly Collective, that... Don't ask, just don't ask okay! That you could possibly live together without sucking each others brains out, or anything else for that matter, but your combined thingy can be harmonized so that together you can achieve great pink flowery 'ahh' type things.

28

SAME GENDER TWINS?

A twin relationship... Relationship even, isn't necessarily between a man and a woman. The polarity of twins is an inner matter, the outer vessel: your wobbly bits (body) may not follow suit. It's not uncommon for a woman to be very masculine or a man to be feminine. Whether they are gay or not is another matter. Indeed many light workers who've evolved beyond the third dimension, no longer have distinct masculine or feminine polarities. Law be 'a' changin beyond tha county line partner!

MEANING OF THE ADAM AND EVE STORY

It is said that Eve was created from Adam, a spare rib with sweet and sour source as it were. Adam and Eve are polarities: Light and Love, masculine and feminine. That Eve was made from Adam is a symbolic reference to the twins being of the same source, the division of a soul. Adam and Eve are not physical people; they are souls or the personalities of such (higher self). They live in paradise: the spiritual realm.

Eve bites into the apple from a sacred tree. This is the tree of life; its branches are paths of experience and the serpent means earthly

wisdom. It coils around the branches gaining
wisdom from the experience each offers.
The serpent is deemed as evil by religion
because religion deems knowledge as evil.
The apple symbolizes Life: Eve is Love,
Adam is Light, the apple is Life (sacred fruit).
Its seed represent the soul, its fruit the soul's
consciousness and the skin is the physical
self. Biting the apple actually means
partaking of life: to incarnate, or as some
may put it: 'banished from paradise'.

Phoenix MacKenzie

Chapter Two

Katrina

Twenty-seven year old Kathy lived with her abusive husband, the father of her youngest daughter, and three of her four children. The year was 1975. A cold and unaffectionate mother and an abusive stepfather, who molested her for many years during her childhood, had raised her. Kathy wanted to stop the abuse; so taking drastic measures she conceived a child at the young age of seventeen, by a local man, her first love. In time she had three more children that lived with her in a secluded valley, while the eldest remained living with her mother. There were five houses in the valley; all were friends and recreational drug users.

One day, while the men and children of the valley were gone, a 'friend' of the group arrived and shared what he called cocaine with three ladies of the group (hoping to get lucky I believe). It turned out the drug was really PCP, an elephant tranquilizer. All three of the ladies got very ill and immediately went to bed. Kathy was in a coma-like state for three days.

Sometime during those three days, Kathy left her body and I, Katrina, stepped in.

When I awoke, later all I remembered was spinning; a head with no body. I looked into the mirror but didn't recognize myself. More shock lay ahead as I found I did not recognize my children or my husband.

I had no memories of Kathy's life at first, but over time, I learned how to access them rather like computer files. I can still roll back the embedded tape and find a memory, if I want to. The problem being, it felt alien, with no emotion, rather like watching a movie because the memories were not mine; they were Kathy's.

I raised Kathy's children; learned the two oldest belonged to Kathy, while the two youngest came in knowing I was going to be here. It was difficult to find and reach a connection with the eldest two, but over time, I became friends with one of them. I am now the proud grandmother of nine children and great grandmother of two precious little girls.

Almost immediately, after entering Kathy's body, I began divorce proceedings. I then felt the extreme urge to research. I took classes and read everything and anything on I could find on spiritual teachings, healings and psychic abilities. I discovered that what had happened to me was called "Walking in" when one soul leaves a body and another one takes its place. During that time I also began having vivid dreams of sitting around in a circle with the Elders, discussing my return to this planet. I did not want to return here, as this planet is one of such pain, suffering and violence but I was promised my Twin-flame to walk hand in hand with me into the ascension, if I agreed to return. My mission was (and still is) to bring love to a cold, heartless planet, which was obsessed with greed. In order for this planet to raise its vibration in preparation for the ascension it needs to learn love, as love is all there is. As it turned out, I was a part of Kathy's soul, living a parallel life that had just completed that lifetime. I was not intended to return to this plane for I had learned all the lessons available for me on this level, but I was needed. I did extensive research on Twin-flames and learned that when souls come into being, issued forth by God/Goddess, they are then separated. Each half has to go forth and learn as much as possible, to raise their vibration in order to be returned to one another. That is why people are constantly searching for something that fits, to make them feel complete.

I spent many years going from one place to another and from one relationship to another, searching and searching. I had knowledge of the 'Other side' (beyond the veil) that most people here did not possess. I brought these memories back with me and didn't lose them, as I would have, had I gone through birth and grown up as most people do. I was thought to be odd; I was very intuitive, did psychic readings and taught classes. I tried to teach people that there is no death, and all there is, is love.

On many occasions, I would meditate and ask my guides where my Twin-flame was and how I would recognize him? I was told he was ill and a couple other personal things to help me recognize him. As it turned out, my husband, my Twin-flame is blind and suffers from diabetes.

Many times over those years, I thought I was crazy and this was all a hallucination. I almost gave up believing in a Twin-flame. Then I would have a dream of a past life spent with my Twin. I always woke with the memory of his intense blue eyes and the feeling of the most overwhelming love.

December 2005, I left another abusive relationship. I swore it would be my last – no more relationships. I would just keep to myself and complete my mission. Then, shortly after Christmas, I joined a spiritual group on a social networking site. I befriended new spiritual people. One, Marcia (Angel Mystic) and I became close. She was very intuitive and told me what she saw. She knew I had not yet met my Twin-Flame in this life. She told me not to give up. When the time was right I would find him and I would know it was him. She too, was searching for her Twin-flame. We became each other's support.

The leader (Guru) of our group, Phoenix was an amazing person. He lived in Scotland and grew up in the mystery schools of Britain. He became my advisor, then my close friend. Neither Marcia nor I could read him; he was guarded, closed down to our intuition. I asked Marcia, what she felt from him and all she would say is that only I would know if he was the person I was looking for.

I remember a deep wrenching, yearning, just before we connected. I truly felt that I would never find him; it was a dark moment, a dark period of emotional cleansing. Then I opened myself up more, became more involved in the group and realized he was right there in front of me. I realized later, after talking with Phoenix and other Twin-flame couples that we had all been through a period of emptiness and emotional cleansing, shortly before we connected with our other half. Many of us have also experienced connecting with a 'near' Twin. One who seems like the one we are looking for, but something just isn't right and usually ends badly.

Strange things began to happen... I would wake at night and see a giant translucent phoenix in my bedroom doorway. Once while I shopped the song 'All by myself' crackled-on the overhead speaker. I cried, for that was my song. I was so tired of being alone without love in my life. Later that day, I saw a phoenix in a cloud formation in the sky, as I sat on my front porch. Everything seemed to point to Phoenix.

We were in constant contact, by phone, messenger or daily email. We learned that we shared our pain or injuries and could heal one another. His frozen left shoulder matched my right shoulder, if I healed my part, he would be healed too – Yin Yang, opposite body parts.

He was in my dreams, dreams that we realized we both shared, as we related them to each other.

I was calm and sure of him. So when he

offered to pay half the price of a ticket to London. I couldn't wait to see him! Before I set out to meet him, on Mother's Day, I was at my daughter's house and her nephew, a tattoo artist, offered me a free tattoo. I chose a Phoenix. When I met my Twin-flame, I saw an identical phoenix on his leg. Mine was on my lower right leg and his on his upper left leg, again the yin-yang.

I had to obtain a passport and pack enough for five weeks, and then came the hard part. I had to tell my kids (who were now grown with children of their own) I was flying to another country to meet a man had I met on the Internet. Instantly I received multiple lectures and warnings but I paid no attention. Nothing could dissuade me; I was so sure this was right.

Phoenix had shared with me that he felt his heart was closed and he could not love another soul, not even his own daughter. He had to remain neutral, teaching and guiding from a place of detachment. Knowing and believing that only his true Twin-flame could open his heart. I wasn't worried. I knew we had a deep connection that was most probably a Twin-flame one.

He was married at the time. A few years before we met, his guides informed him that his Twin-flame was in Northern California. He had met another woman (his near Twin) in Oregon, just above Northern California. He sold all of his belongings, went to Oregon and married her. She wanted to live in Scotland. Sharing a lifetime there, she felt it was her true home. In a previous lifetime, he had rescued her in a battle in Scotland; she was royalty and he a soldier. He had a spiritual contract to help her return there. Six months down the line, she moved into the spare room declaring she did not love him, but wanted to remain in Scotland.

After finally making it through immigration. I swear the woman was personally offended by me for some reason. I was asked a multitude of questions and then made to sit in a chair for twenty minutes while she tried to reach Phoenix on the phone. Finally I reached him and as he put his arms around me, I felt like I had come home. A few days later I knew it was time to open his heart; I knelt down before him and placed a crystal over his heart. I poured all my love and energy into the clear stone. A gargoyle-like electric guardian hovered over us; a claw pierced my forehead as it settled on my head. It was his protector making sure he was not being harmed. After the ceremony ended, he changed. His love flowed to his daughter and he began to smile during precious moments while watching children play in the local park. His heart was now open.

The next three years was destined for us to be apart; we carried our love on in a long distance relationship. Then in 2007, I spent six months with Phoenix, in Scotland while awaiting the divorce from his near Twin. In June 2008, he flew to the United States and we married. Later, I joined him in Wales in September, after awaiting the birth of my youngest grandson.

My Twin-flame and I have been married for five years. We have met other Twin-flame couples and I have decided to write this book to assist others who are searching for their Twin.

My husband and I are both writers. I write children's books, paranormal/romance and spiritual books. He writes science fiction and fantasy for adults, which incorporate spiritual messages within. We are both very spiritual; we teach and do readings for others. It is interesting that I read Tarot intuitively and he reads from analyzing the symbols, but the readings come out the same.

Our life together is calm and centered. We are best friends and share everything. We rarely go out and are together twenty-four hours a day. We fit, where one of us shows weakness the other shows strength. We both collect gemstones, statues and boxes. We are both drawn to Egyptian art, Indian art and Mythology. We would live in a crystal cave if we could. Most of our days are spent sitting on our twin computers, separated by a fireplace, writing our books. I also do crafty things, like making gemstone jewelry, knitting, etc. Due to the fact that we both have illnesses, he was born with Type 1 Diabetes and I have developed Dercum's Disease since my arrival in Wales, we have lots of affection in our relationship, but not as much sexual activity as we did at the beginning.

Most reports you'll find on Twin-flame couple's push the fact that the relationship is all about love and sex, but that is not true. Yes the sex can be amazing (I never dreamed that my body would vibrate when he touched me intimately), but Twin-flames come together for a higher purpose and that is to serve humanity in some way. If nothing else, the unconditional love they share is, and will be an example of true love, which is what the world needs today.

How do you find your Twin-flame? Well you can manifest them, but the best thing you can do is work on yourself. Get all your issues resolved. Let go of your past and prepare for a future by yourself, you can do it you are strong enough. Then, if your Twin is incarnated, they will come to you. It is predestined, planned before you incarnated here between the two of you.

Chapter Three

Phoenix

Katrina and I became friends on Myspace as we shared common spiritual interests. I ran a small group that meditated together once a week: for the purpose of healing Earth and its 'grid'. This 'grid work' took place at an ancient vantage point, a plane of existence that dwells in another dimension. Like gravity it surrounds, flows through space and time as an ocean of consciousness manifested by the sacred thoughts and visions of countless minds through eons of time. Here in a limitless expanse are forests, temples, oceans, rivers, mountains and many forms of life. Into it Earth and other realms can be summoned for healing.

We gathered there expressing our more 'native' forms, that is to say: expressions of life that have had a dominant influence over our spiritual evolution. Light workers are usually from other realms aside from Earth. They may resemble angels or what are deemed 'mythical creatures' by humans, such as mermaids and fairies. It is something within us that prompts the stories told through the ages, a collective consciousness often wrongly termed 'imagination'.

Within a forest surrounding a crystal hedge, Katrina joined this gathering for the first time, at least in this incarnation. She recognized other people amongst our group and met some of those who join us from many realms, often very angelic. Then Katrina saw me in one of a variety of forms I express. If I remember correctly I was half man, half bird, half physical, half energy/fire at the time. At that moment she recognized me as her twin and fell to her knees. Others in our group distracted her, drawing Katrina away, dancing and socializing as we used to before gathering in a circle to become channels of Love: directed toward the Earth. The first experience of this sacred place can be confusing or overwhelming. Katrina's reaction was put down to this and nothing said of what she felt, as I was married at the time.

I'd known that my twin lived in America for sometime and searched there for her. At first I met a young woman online who also studied with the Rosicrucian Order. We had a very strong bond, past life connections and so forth. I travelled to the East coast and stayed with her wonderful family for several weeks. However, any romantic connection was lost almost instantly. While love bound us, as with a past life we were brother and sister to each other: soul family. It turned out that my mission was to aid her sister through a difficult time in her life, healing deep pain from several lifetimes. I returned to England feeling used and manipulated by my higher self.

This helped to provoke a turning point in my life, which from an early age had been devoted to the cause of Light. I'd studied to high levels of esoteric teaching, though none of it was new to me and I began to write discourses for the ancient Order I'd studied with. My own desires had been only to serve. I travelled to America again and venues in Britain: sharing what my soul furnished, conducting psychic experiments. The demands of such led to a stroke, my face was paralysed. Therefore I could no longer lecture. Although also blind I could see so much, even my soul personality (soul consciousness, the 'I' of countless lifetimes) and yet I could not see my twin. A Master in India had said I would see 'her' and with it the dawn would come. I moved away from my mystical family and town that I'd grown up in, beginning a new life of just living: being around 'ordinary' people. This was quite amusing as people in Hastings were far from ordinary. The usual relationships failed, what with me being from another planet an all. I just don't understand these human women: press relationship button and things start to get weird; friends are great, lots of fun, but relationships - scary stuff. A long and somewhat insane story!

Years later I returned to America, my third visit. This time to the West coast: Oregon and California to meet the woman who would become my second wife. Again we had such a strong connection, in both this and past lives. Little did I know that my true twin was so close and the connection to my second wife was another soul contract: an oath made many lifetimes ago. It should be said that through this relationship I discovered more about my past and started to balance my desire to help others and keep the peace at all costs, with the ability to confront and stand up for myself as much as I would for other people. She aided in this difficult, unpleasant lesson and I furnished her with the means to return to Scotland where she'd once been part of the Pictish Matriarchy.

I'd moved from a town on the south coast of England: Hastings and now lived in the far north, highlands of Scotland with my second wife. 'Lived with' is all the short marriage had become and I was of no mind to seek another relationship at that time or for the foreseeable future. I valued friendship and found this a source of true love and companionship, rather than romantic inclinations. My marriage was yet another spiritual contract made between soul mates that I mistook for my twin flame. Such feelings I had for them and such a connection: how could I be so wrong? Indeed I felt wronged by my own cold calculating soul, that's will it seemed I was a slave to. I'd grown resentful of this 'higher' manipulation, servitude to the greater good or greater something. This again was a turning point in life, my existence here on Earth, this duality. Slavery in any form is wrong and so many conversations took place between myself and I, the crux of which boiled down to: 'you come down here to the physical and experience it first hand THEN determine a path in life', which is actually an ongoing process at the moment.

My woes were shared with close spiritual friends, such as Katrina, who, knowing my marriage had failed, then expressed how she felt about me. Oh crap here we go again, but what if? We began meeting on the astral plane before meeting in the physical. We met in the physical realm in England. Katrina flew over from California and we stayed at my brother's apartment in Hastings: an historical seaside resort. Hastings is a town close to our heart, filled with characters: poets, artists, writers and die hard hippies, though somewhat spoiled by drunks and drug addicts. My brother's small apartment was nestled at the base of cliffs upon which perched the ruins of an old castle. From its balcony one can be inspired by ocean views and life passing by.

Given my state of mind Katrina was well aware she'd a job on her hands convincing me she was who she thought: that we were Twin Flames. There was no way in Hell or Earth for that matter I was listening to any 'inner' guidance on this, been there, done that and there's no refunds! I knew that only my Twin could resurrect my heart, a heart sacrificed many lives ago to ease the way of my spiritual work. Human emotions can cloud our perception; the spiritual path can be harsh and testing at times. To be a guardian and guide along such, to walk it over and over again with one seeker after another requires metaphorical sturdy walking boots, not flip-flops. In this life alone I'd faced death, walked amongst lepers, other people rotting in the street from malnutrition or disease, abject poverty and so on. Many lives of such experience can make one numb to what we deem as 'suffering' in this day and age. "Oh my X-Box is broken, woe ist me".

Aware of the healing task before her, Katrina knelt in front of me as I sat in a chair. She began to perform healing on my heart and as expected this aroused the attention of a guardian. We both heard its gigantic wings before it entered the apartment. Katrina's hair began to stand on end as the gargoyle-like electric blue guardian approached behind me. Grasping Katrina's head with one hand it pierced her forehead (third eye) with a claw. At that point she projected herself within my heart. I could feel her there: continuing to heal. I could see her holding up a crystalline light; this was the 'cell' or 'gem', the 'souls scribe' that dwells within our hearts. Only another soul of our 'prime resonance' our twin can touch this, as if it were our own soul, which a Twin is. The process was quite agonizing for me, as if shards of a broken crystal were being set back in place within my chest.

I began to experience feelings over the following weeks and months, alien to me: human emotions. The antics and cute ways of children made me smile for the first time in many lives. Until then people were very much like they are depicted in The Matrix movie: sequences of numbers - cause and effect, karma, energy streams. I was more akin to a computer: analyzing. My feeling restricted to what was right and just, Honor and the 'whys' of everything that happens to people. Now compassion, little things in life, living in the moment merged with my sense of being.

However, with this came a darkness, feelings conspired with all the 'whys' I knew, nurturing a seed of discontent with the 'way of things'. My gaze turned to the architects of 'the way' here on Earth, that suffering was a foul teacher not worthy of those who are meant to provide a path to unity and Love. Indeed a rumble stirred within my 'spiritual' kin (race), who are known for their powers of both creation and destruction.

Katrina returned to America after five weeks and I returned to Scotland. We both had to face the 'hows' of getting together and the great, somewhat extortionate expense of immigration paperwork. As my divorce was going through, Katrina and I continued to visit. It was my turn to meet her family in the States, traveling from California to Nevada. I had pride of place in the weirdo exhibition, what with being from another planet called Europe and talking funny. Katrina then visited me in Scotland, where the Masters of talking funny live, for as long as immigration would allow. I wanted to spend as much time with her as possible, not only for obvious reasons, but also to make sure we would get along together. That she didn't want to burn my home down, accuse me of dark sinister plotting, having affairs with imaginary women and so on and so forth... Been there, done that.

Although twins are of the same 'seed' they may be separated for so long. Time loses meaning. Evolving amongst different cultures, different forms of life, perhaps only incarnating together once in a thousand years. Therefore our ways can be very different despite that core resonance that binds us. Our souls try to prepare the way, often enlisting the aid of soul mates and soul family, which can mean painful experiences, heartbreak, changes and in the meantime what seems like a hopeless search for each other.

Finally I flew to America for our marriage, encountering the charm of American immigration that victimized everyone on the flight who had a disability (I'm blind). As a result a woman had her luggage stolen while we were detained. That was the last time I would endure the attitude of immigration people who like to play god and treat people as if they are dirt. This has been a common problem for Twins trying to get together, as if the dark tyrannical forces are trying to prevent such union. There was little time to prepare for, and scarce finance to provide the wedding we would have liked, but it was a nice setting in Carson City and the guests provided a very charming... Okay I'll be honest they were all nuts, but in a nice way, I mean hey: they were Katrina's friends and family, they gotta be crazy people!

So after many years of searching for each other and lifetimes apart we were finally together. I think a lot of people expect the world to stop moving when meeting their twin, that all will be 'just so'. My life has been a sequence of what some may deem 'miracles' or perhaps 'strange phenomena' and therefore I'm perhaps not so 'moved' by what is to most people 'unusual', to me, what Katrina and I are to each other is 'comfortable'. We've known each other for a long time after all. The differences between us are like missing pieces of a jigsaw puzzle once brought together we are complete. For instance I am patient in ways Katrina is not, she is patient in ways I'm not. I am intuitive in ways she isn't and she's intuitive in ways I'm not. If we are going somewhere new Katrina wants a map and stresses if we step one foot without confirming a street name. I just follow my nose. Katrina reads Tarot cards intuitively; I analyze the symbols, colors and features of the Tarot language. We reach the same conclusion, but in different ways: masculine and feminine.

Katrina can be quite masculine in some respects and I can be quite feminine. I love grace, flow, elegance and sensuality. Katrina likes sweatshirts, banging nails in the wall and 'just get to the point man'. On the other hand I'm a Master Carpenter and like to construct things, creatively I'm methodical. Katrina creates 'pretty things' and has enough stinky stuff to supply a legion of fairies... Fairies that like perfume, body lotion and other items, I categorize as 'stink' that is. We'd be perfect if mushed together as one person, but that's just it: we are one person, two halves of one soul.

Our political views are very similar: socialist, as in social (of and for the people) - ism. Personally I cannot see how someone can be a capitalist and call themselves spiritual. That's not to say we are communist though, got to be room for people to be what they want to be, but not insanely rich while others live in poverty. Balance is the key to life.

There's seventeen years, physically speaking,

between us: my wife is older than I, although her being a 'Walk-in' complicates this. Therefore she has spent fewer years here than I have; it is only the body she adopted that is older than mine. (She walked into this life sometime after I was born.) My body also ages much faster as I've had diabetes since I was an infant. Katrina and I both have very debilitating conditions: I've had diabetes since 1966 and Katrina has Dercums, so we don't get out as much as we'd like to. We have an office rather than a living room and that's where we spend every waking hour: at our computers, one either side of a fireplace.

We're both authors, Katrina writing Paranormal Romance, while I write what might be termed Paranormal Science Fiction. We both write Fantasy: Katrina for children and I write for adults who still have a child within them, a naughty child that might break free any moment! Yesss, you can feel him/her in there can't you; just itching to do something naughty when no one's looking.

Spiritually speaking we'd both live in a crystal cave if possible. So if you know of any sparkly caves with central heating and Internet access do let us know. We're polytheists which means our perspective of God/dess is a universal force or consciousness, that God/dess is everything:

you, me, sky and the tree, stars, cars, Venus and Mars, chocolate and... Well you get the picture. We're both Reiki Masters with the view that Reiki is some modern name for something we already knew and practiced. We're an old soul with some grumpy ways, preferring ancient methods over new age, which are at times simply a dilution and corruption of ancient systems.

We're pretty much of a mind spiritually with one major exception. I detest belief and encourage 'knowing', not necessarily study and intellect, but let's just say a cat is a cat, you don't have to believe it's a cat, that's what it is. I think I'm that way as I've had a formal mystical education and so many 'psychic experiences' in life why would I ever need to believe in what is factual? Katrina still used the term 'believe' perhaps because she talks to people who have little knowledge or experience with psychic/spiritual concepts, phenomena and domains. She deals with the intuitive more than I do. However, we are both of the opinion that religion has done so much harm to the world and spiritual evolution. As far as I'm concerned terms like belief and praying belong to a religious era that needs to be dead and buried.

It takes time and tolerance to learn how to work together, especially two old cranky farts like us. Not just in the sense of living under the same roof, but also how to blend psychic/spiritual abilities. How opposing opinions are often little more than different perceptions of the same thing. I wouldn't say there's an Earth shattering, blockbuster movie mission in life for us; we don't pretend to be the great guru's and such. Katrina and I simply love to help people understand more as we go along.

I think the greatest strengths of our unified flame are sanctuary, sanctity and our own brand of sanity. (Special offer on S words today, get them while stocks last!) Our home and life together provide solace from the hordes of zombies and financial vampires out there. We are aliens on a strange and primitive... I hesitate to say 'world' as Earth is far from primitive, it is the slavish societies in which humans live: lives given over for no other reason than adding wealth to a few greedy, insanely rich 'people'. I relate to Phoenix mythology when I think of us: the gathering of our elements to form a nest, set afire (purified) by life (the sun). There an egg (sanctuary, unified consciousness) forms and from it a serpent (wisdom) rises, transforming into a new Phoenix.

Chapter Four

Natasha and Michael

We met as friends on myspace. Michael sent a friend request, and after that, we communicated through comments and short messages. Each of us felt a connection to the other, like we had met in a past life or something, although, we had no idea what the connection was at that time. We shared similar ideas and beliefs, and knew that we wanted to stay in touch. At the time we met online, we were both married to other people, not looking for romance or relationships, just friends. I turned 35 in February, and Michael will be 41 in June.

I was the oldest of three children. My mother had me when she was 16, and my grandparents adopted me at the age of 2. My sisters lived with my mother and their father, and at 15, I went to live with them until they divorced in 1992. Mom was strict and religious, as were my grandparents, but she was not as strict as they were. After Mom and my stepfather divorced, we moved to another state. We were always a close family; Mom, sisters, my grandparents and -me until this event. Mom and my sisters returned to Mississippi after living here one year due to a decline in my grandparents' health. Since Mom and I were not on good terms at that point, I decided to remain in Arkansas. (I met my biological father only once at the age of 20.) We were once a very loving and supportive family, and although I love them still, we are all very different, whereas we used to be so similar. I barely know my sisters anymore, and one of them; I have not talked to in over a year. Mom and I grew apart after our beliefs clashed so much, but we talk once or twice a week on the phone. She married a man about 12 years ago who clashes with everything we believe, think, and do. That single incident has driven a distinct wedge in the family relationship, and I have lived 500 miles away from my family for years now, and do not feel the urgency to be back together. I have managed to adopt a lifestyle of independence apart from my family. The rest of them still live in the same town and are close, the antics of my mother's husband (not my sisters' father, this is another guy) are overlooked or excused just to keep things that way. That is a game I grew tired of playing.

I feel I am the queen of bad relationships, lol. That's terrible. There always seemed to be strange conditions that brought me into my previous relationships, but I know that each and every one of them taught me valuable life lessons. My dating history was a train wreck waiting to happen, and my first marriage ended because he beat our firstborn son to death. (This is something I have not mentioned earlier, because it is such a private and painful part of my life.) My second husband was a great friend that should have never been a husband. We got along really well, mostly, but there were issues with trust and sexuality that caused a deep divide in our relationship. My last marriage was all about pain and deep buried emotions, emotional abuse, and control. I was going through another last swing of rebellious behavior when I began that relationship with Emilio, and now see the value of things learned from it. My relationship with Michael is not comparable to any of my previous relationships, and everything has been dramatically different. With Michael, everything has been wonderful. There is so much Love, Peace, and Freedom. It is hard to put into words just how wonderful our relationship is.

About a month before I realized Michael as my twin flame, Emilio, my ex husband, wanted to have another child. He saw that as another way to bind me to him, and insure that I would continue to need him around, although he was very aware that things were tense and strained. I was against the crazy idea, but had reluctantly stopped using any method of contraception. I had missed my period. I was about two weeks late. I was beginning to suspect that I might be pregnant, and about that time, I had a very vivid dream. I was with one of the Elders. The Elder was seated at a desk that supported a holographic image rising out of the center of it. I was standing before the Elder, who appeared to be a woman, but not sure about that, as they seem to have no gender.

Anyway, the Elder said to look at the hologram. It appeared as a 'tree' with a distinct split, where the branches went in opposite directions from the trunk. It was explained, although words were not used, that this represented where I was at this point in time. I had a choice. One path, I would have a baby, and continue on the same path in my marriage. The second option was 'LOVE', nothing elaborated on, no details, those were the options. In my thinking, I said (telepathically) well, if all stays as it is in my life, and a child is born into it, it could be disastrous. However, if I chose LOVE, you just cannot go wrong with Love. It seems I was waiting for a response or approval that I was making the right choice, but the Elder remained quite expressionless, as it was my choice to make, and I was not being influenced one way or the other. "She" asked telepathically was that my choice? I answered YES. The Elder almost smiled, it seemed, but was as if I was not supposed to see that..? Anyway, the dream ended. The very next day, I started my period, and was one of the heaviest I ever remember having. I instantly remembered the dream, and thought it was very important. Not long after, major life events happened that threw me directly onto a path filled with the most intense and incredible Love I have ever known, and I realized Michael as my Twin Flame!

I had to love myself. That took a long time to be able to do that. I realized that the love I sought was not external; it was in my own heart. That was what gave me the strength to let go of my struggling marriage. I just released it back into the universe, and said 'thank you for showing me that'. Emilio was a marriage of tough love, and constant emptiness. I had to find it within myself

I have also had a 5 or 10 second 'vision' or remembrance of sorts of being with Michael in a past life. Seemed to be the 1700's, and we lived near the sea, he was a seaman on a merchant ship. I remember saying goodbye, and the feeling that it was the last time I would see him, that he never came home. THAT 'vision' was so terrible and powerful, I was in tears and greatly moved by it.

Michael flew to the US six months after we realized we were Twin-flames. We were online friends approximately six months before we figured it out. Michael sent me a blog that someone had posted about Twin-flames on myspace, and until that moment, I had never heard much about Twin-flames. I had actually left a comment for Michael the very same day that he sent the blog, and the image was titled, "Twin Soul". I assumed the he understood the image, and sent me information on that subject due to the image in the comment. Turns out, he had no idea of the connection of the blog and image until I brought it up a few weeks after! One of those coincidences that seem to happen in surprising numbers. (We have found that synchronicity is quite common with Twin-flames.) Michael felt that we might be Twin-flames, and thought it a bold move to send me the information. He had no idea how I would respond to it. As I read the description of Twin-flames and the information in that blog, tears streamed down my face and I knew in that instant Michael was my Twin. Everything fit perfectly. At that time, I KNEW, but was wondering if HE knew, or was just sharing information on a very interesting subject!

My marriage was falling apart for the last year and a half that we were together. Within realizing that Michael was my twin, doors just opened, and things fell apart, as if a new pathway was opening up before me! It seems that things could have ended at any moment in the last year and a half, and after realizing my twin had been found. or he found me.. Things just dissolved rather rapidly! Seemed to be surreal how it all happened, and Emilio and I separated in August 07, after about a year and a half of trying to maintain a severely crippled marriage. (Michael and Sue separated about September 07.) Before we even met, we loved each other and wanted to be together. Mike stayed for two weeks in Dec 07-Jan 08, and returned in June 08 for four weeks. During that time, my divorce was finalized (June 24, 08) and Michael and I were married on June 28, 2008. He had to return again to the UK, and came back to the US again for 3 weeks in October 08. Since then, we have been apart, and that has been very difficult for the both of us.

We have a lot of similar beliefs and ideas, we

seem to be on the same Spiritual path, and like many of the same things like nature, the Celtic/Wiccan tradition, similar taste in music, and, ironically, we were both adopted. (My grandparents adopted me at the age of 2, although I always allowed a relationship with my mother. We were very close. Mike was adopted and never knew his birth parents.)

Both of us feel a strong call to serve humanity in some way, and feel that our lives and coming together have a Divine Purpose. We are both Vegetarians. We both had black vehicles, until Mike sold his last November. We speak the same language, and neither of us have a brother. We were both married before we met. We both have an interest in the unusual, unexplained, UFOs and the paranormal. We are both the oldest child of the family.

Due to geographic location, we have a very different idea about food, but that was to be expected. I have two boys from my previous marriage, and Michael has no children (although he quite readily claims my boys!). Michael questioned authority and standardized systems of structure from a much earlier age than I. Michael had no real ties to religion (although he attended a church school for about 5 years), but I was made to go to church and had religion crammed down my throat for as long as I lived under my mother's roof, yet attended public schools from start to finish. Michael excelled in Science and Physics, although my best subjects were literature and art. I have been an on and off again smoker throughout my life. Mike has never smoked.

My relationship with Michael is not comparable to any of my previous relationships, and everything has been dramatically different. With Michael, everything has been wonderful. There is so much Love, Peace, and Freedom. It is hard to put into words just how wonderful our relationship is. The way we communicate, the openness, the bond, the freedom. There are not feelings of control, jealousy, pain, or anything like that. I love him completely with all my heart and soul, and although that is a cliché in relationships- that one loves with all their heart and soul, until it is experienced, there is no real idea of how that actually feels. Making love with Michael literally blows the top off my crown chakra, and EVERY CELL of my being participates and explodes into crystal particles of light with orgasm! It is amazing, and I never imagined anything like it. The entire process is a devotion to love and each other. It is the most beautiful thing I have experienced. It is not just a physical sensation, as it was in previous relationships, but a full experience of the BEING, the spirit, the energy field, the mind, the heart, and the body, like a fine tuned instrument being played by the hand of The Creator! WOW!

We are daily reminders for each other that miracles do happen. We are a support for each other in so many ways, and we are truly best friends. We can talk about anything. Michael has always had the ability to clear away the storm clouds when I was feeling down, and he reminds me often of my Divinity. He says I draw him into the light, although, I am quite sure he was already there ;).

Do we have a mission together, I still wonder this myself! I get the impression that it is to help return the world to Love and Harmony. To help teach others about a higher and more fulfilling type of love and relationship...to assist in the Earth's Ascension. The Elders spoke to me in a dream and said that we MUST tell the world about Twin-Flames and give the message of LOVE in any way possible.

His visa was recently approved, and he is finishing up some last minute things before his appointment with the Embassy. The plan is to fly 'home' to the US in June 09.

UPDATE- May 2013

The day that Mike had his appointment with the embassy, and the day we THOUGHT he was going to get approval for a VISA was the worst day ever. When Mike was 19 years old, he loaned his car to a friend who went and got fuel at a few places around town and did not have the money to pay for it.

He left "collateral" until he could go back and pay for the fuel. At one place, he left a spare tire - at the next, a car stereo, and so on. Although Mike did not commit the crimes, he was aware that his friend did this, so was considered a co-conspirator. He had to go to court and pay a fine. This was considered payment for the offense, and he never thought another thing about it. When he entered the country in Dec 2007, June 2008, and Oct 2008, he came on a passport and a waiver. He had to sign a form each time that said he had never been convicted of a crime. Since he did not disclose this incident on any of the 3 accounts, they said he was guilty of moral turpitude. So his visa was cancelled and he was denied entrance to the US for the next two years

It was a dark time for both of us. Our

immigration attorney that we had used up to this point said he could not help us any farther in the process, and referred us to another attorney. She was quite expensive, but had a 99% success rate and could do a VISA waiver case. She told us it would be at least 12-18 months AFTER she had all the required information to submit to immigration.

We were heartbroken, disgruntled, and missing each other like crazy. We had always talked every night on SKYPE for hours at a time. As it was, this was all we had, and all that we were going to have for a very, VERY long time. Several months in, the separation and desperation were really taking a toll on us. I found that all I could do was cry and I felt sad all the time. I found myself looking for distractions to the pain. I found that alcohol eased a lot of my pain, as well as sleeping more than usual. I finally sought help for my depression and was put on anti-depressants and anti-anxiety meds. On the medications, I could function, but I felt numb. I felt nothing. It was better than crying all the time, but I felt dead. Mike really didn't know what to do, since he was away from me against his will, and I could not go to him, due to travel expenses. There were times I didn't know if I could wait another year or 18 months. I live 500 miles away from my closest family, and I truly felt cut off from everyone I loved - just my two children and me.

I had doubts if we were both strong enough to stay on the path. As part of my distractions, I made a few male friends that I talked to on chat on facebook. Mike had met some new women friends. It wasn't long before karmic behaviors were manifesting on both sides, and that is when it **REALLY** got messy. I questioned everything, was this right? Was I wrong about the twin flame connection? Were we still going to want to be together after all this blew over? Was it worth it in the end for all that we were going through, all the loneliness and pain and broken trust? I still wasn't really feeling anything, so I stopped taking the medications. Slowly, I started to feel again. It took a while, but I came to my senses and realized that I already knew the answers to all my questions.

What Mike and I have together is unparalleled to anything I have ever known. He is the yin to my yang - the hand to my glove - I was **CRAZY** to think that it was ok to just walk away and stop trying. In November 2010, he went back to the embassy for the visa interview. This time, all went well, and he was granted entry to the US. Within a month, he was on a flight back to the US. FINALLY! All the waiting and persistence had paid off.

We have been going strong ever since, and we are so happy that neither of us gave up on it working out. Sometimes, I am in such awe of him that I get all teary eyed, and I remember just how fortunate I am to have found my twin flame.

I can see how one could become disillusioned about twins and how it works. I'd say to anyone looking for their TF: you must love yourself first. You must start there. Clear out all the negativity and release it. Your twin will come when you least expect it. I didn't even know what a TF was until I met Mike. When things are in balance, it will manifest. I've seen so many searching and looking for their TF and wondering with each relationship, "Is this the one?"
Both Twins have to be at a certain vibrational level, understanding that LOVE is the answer to everything. It's like discovering a magic key to unlock a hidden door in the matrix. All things will happen when the timing is right.

Chapter Five

Amy and Skip

Before I ever met my darling hubby, I saw him in a vision shortly after I woke up from my drug overdose. I was lying in my hospital bed, and drifted into unconsciousness. I vividly remember walking along a rocky ocean beach, hand in hand with a HUGE blonde guy with a shaved head and tattoos. The vision was from behind, and this man was easily 10" taller than I was. I also knew from this dream that he was my husband. (My husband at the time was an dark Italian guy, only about 6'0." It definitely wasn't him, reminded me of my brother...) I remember my best friend being near my bedside, and I told her about this "weird dream" I had about holding hands with a guy who looked a lot like my brother. But I knew I loved him. I remember the sky being dark purple in the dream, too.

Shortly after I awoke from my coma, I spent another couple weeks in ICU and then spent a week in medical detox. This facility was located in another county and a place I'd never heard of before. My room-mate in detox was a woman named Mary.

Mary and I were both discharged from detox the same day--a full week-ish earlier then either of us had expected (she was a rich, 50+ year old alcoholic, I was a 26 year old pill-popper), but we had similar medical insurance coverage and they booted us out after only a few days (most people stayed in for 30 days or more).

A few days after returning home from detox, I was enrolled (not by choice) to an outpatient drug-rehab program in the next town. It was an intensive program--three hours per night ever night for at least 30 days. I walked into the current group (only six members), and my detox-roommate Mary was sitting there. It was also her first night. It made me so immediately comfortable I decided to stay to see what "rehab" would be like.

And then a 6'5, " tattooed guy with a shaved head walked into the room. And I almost puked.

Weirdly enough, he, Skip, and I lived less than two miles from each other.

Skip and I started attending our requisite NA or AA meetings, and I picked him up one day at his home. It turned out he lived on the exact same cul-de-sac (only a few doors down) from the childhood home of my then husband (now ex-husband). My son now plays with the little boys that live in my ex-husband's boyhood home. Needless to say, when the split happened, between me and my ex (and I left him to live with Skip), it was very difficult for my ex to deal with the whole neighborhood issue. He took it very personally, but it was really just "coincidence."

I think he and I always had a strange draw to one another after meeting for the first time. Our friendship was very deep, very quick. But because I was married, we held back the affection part for a long time. He would hang out with my husband and I (which didn't last too long), and I used to befriend his prospective girlfriends (including another woman named Mary...)

We're married now and expecting a baby in August.
I overdosed in 12/06 and we met in late 01/07. Our "relationship" really got moving

my 5/07 and I left my then-husband and moved in with Skip 12/07.

Skip is two years older than me. He is a Scorpio and I am a Taurus.

We were both at our absolute worst point. I was vehemently agnostic still, and remember having to perform my "second step" in-group in front of him, where I acknowledged a power greater than myself. I refused to, even though I had just undergone my whole Near Death Experience and didn't understand what the hell I had just seen. He was in a horrible place as well. I think we were both blank slates, as far as spiritual beliefs were concerned. We were also raised very differently--he was from Utah and raised Mormon, I was from the Pacific Northwest and raised Protestant.

We have many synchronicities; Skip's middle name is Ward, which is my last name/maiden name (I never changed my last name with my first marriage--in fact, my ex-husband took my last name and my son still has my last name). The Ward name is a family name for him as well, and it is likely he and I are related somehow.

When we had routine pregnancy blood work

done, our son tested positive for Trisomy-18, which is a birth defect from a glitch in DNA. Our son ended up being fine (after a lot of stressful testing, genetic counseling, etc), but we were informed his likelihood of the Trisomy was due to us being genetically similar.

As for similar and dissimilar tastes, he's got much more of a sweet tooth, but we like pretty much the same thing. We have common taste in music. We don't watch many movies, or TV for that matter. I got my ex-husband's giant flat screen in the divorce. We might as well use it as a plant stand (the kids like it, though).

Similar activities- we are both sex fiends. Neither one of us wants dogs, but we've pooled our cats together and have a pet snake we've named Snakey.

Do you have a mission to complete together? Please explain. Yes. It has to do with our children (we will have four kids under age 10 by the end of this year. God help us.) It is only a small part of our missions, individually. But collectively, our family has our work rooted in the Ascension. Skip and I are both aware of it.

We both had children before meeting. I have a four year old son and he has two daughters (ages 9 and 7), I am also pregnant with a little boy we are naming Elijah. Our son, Elijah, was meant to be. He has an important job to do. Don't know what it is yet, but he kicks a lot.

Skip's daughters and I have always been close and very loving since the beginning. Ironically, I am have been forcefully separated from them by their biological mother, who has informed the courts I am emotionally and verbally abusive to the girls. We are currently embroiled in a HORRIBLE custody battle with their mother. Skip and my son get along fine. Skip's daughters were the first to teach my son to talk. The three kids are all very close and already call each other brother/sister.

How long from the time you connected until you knew you were Twin-flames?
After I truly understood what "twin-flame" meant. All I knew is he was meant to be in my life, one way or another. I NEEDED him.

Update-

Elijah will be four years old in a few months, and so much has happened since those tumultuous years when Skip and I first got married. Not always good things, but transformative to our relationship. It seems that our marriage has been built backwards-- we started with chaos; our divorces, custody battles, instant children,
instant family, and THEN we got married.

Since Eli was born, Skip and I have not been able to focus solely on our relationship, but our relationship has really become the foundation of our family. Through the criminal trials, the family court saga, and the many issues with his ex-wife, we took some of the tenderness and the love for granted, I think. We just assumed it was always there, and didn't make an effort to work on "us." There has never been the time or the resources available to concentrate on the connection we had with one another. And then, when Elijah was two, Skip and I witnessed a man die horrifically in a motorcycle accident. The aftermath of the trauma and the nightmares put us both into counseling, and I suddenly saw a very delicate, human side to my husband. We had a few rough nights that year, dealing with some of our fears and dark shadows.

One particularly bad night, I looked up at Skip and was startled to see myself reflected in his eyes. Instead of seeing his anger, I saw empathy. I realized Skip is no easier to love than I am, and that we promised to love each other in good times and in bad, and this too would pass. We moved shortly after witnessing the cyclist's death to a home, ironically, a block away from the accident scene. Sometimes I feel like the cyclist's spirit is a daily reminder not to take for granted the people I love. Skip and I made serious life changes...we downsized and gave away many of our possessions, stopped watching TV, and began to focus on each other (as much as possible, with up to four kids at a time!). Realizing now that we are getting older and need to take better care of ourselves, we changed our diet and began growing our own vegetables in our yard at the new home. Skip, having never been much of a gardener, realized he found a lot of peace and therapy in the garden...something I had known and enjoyed for years. Together we began raising flowers and vegetables from seed which has transformed our home's outdoor space in amazing ways. Encouraged by this, we began tending gardens at the local nursing home and received many thanks from the residents.

It seemed everywhere our plants would go, it would make someone's day brighter. We were hooked at that point, and have spent the past two years exploring and producing amazing plants for ourselves, our family and friends, two different nursing homes, corporate clients, private clients, schools, and gardens around the city.

Since Skip works around death and illness, he found the ability to create and nurture life to be therapeutic for him. For me, it became a career and I was hired on professionally at an amazing local landscaping company. With word-of-mouth recommendations and help from social media, Skip and I have been able to take on private clients together, and have helped us sustain our family financially through our shared passion. We have also found that we share the same views and goals on the environment, and together we have tried to make an impact not only in our own home, but also in our neighborhood and state as well. Skip has changed the refuse policy at his job to the point that his co-workers jokingly call him "Captain Planet." As his proud and loving "Eco-Queen," he sends my heart soaring for the good he is able to do to the world. I love nothing more than loving and supporting him. He is my best friend, my partner, and my inspiration.

When people talk of "Twin-flames," there is
the romanticized version...that the
two are partners and the relationship is
perfect. It's far from that. He brings out my
shadows and helps me face them. I know
and understand his weaknesses, but he trusts
me not to exploit them. As we have evolved
together, we have grown stronger and more
in love than I would have imagined was
possible.

Now, in the early mornings when we are
waking up, he is stroking my forehead or
touching my cheek, whispering "I love you" in
my ear when he thinks I am sleeping, I feel
so complete, satisfied and happy. There are
no regrets about the path we took to get here.
We clawed and scraped at our chance to be
together, and now we can embrace one
another into our future. He challenges me to
be a better woman, and I have been honored
to help support him into being the man he is
destined to be.

Home is being wrapped in his arms and
listening to the kids play and laugh. It doesn't
matter where we are...the house, the beach,
or the grocery store.
Home is together with him.

Chapter Six

Cindy and Heath

I feel there are many people we meet throughout our lives who capture our hearts. As we look back over the years with those people, we know that although they may have had our heart, loved them and built a life together, there was always an empty space somewhere deep inside that stopped our soul from truly being happy.

I feel the reason for this is that although there are many that may capture our heart for a certain amount of time, there is only one that captures our soul that lasts forever. There is a connection so deep and so lasting, they will always be part of the same entity no matter how much time passes or how much distance is between them. When that happens, it may be we never know and therefore never understand why we have this "hole in our soul", that empty, sad space, somewhere deep inside. We do not realize it is the one who captures our soul that gives us the "whole in our soul". If we have lost them, before we understood this that empty space will always be there, unless we find them again. And when we do know, even if they are not in our lives, we never, ever forget them. The connection is always there.

Twin-flames allow each other to grow they are usually the best of friends and seem to know each other's thoughts and feelings. There seems to be a glow around them that comes from deep inside, which it does, deep within their souls. No matter where they are, they still "feel" each other. Their lives are rich and full. Twin-flames are soul mates that belong in the same spiritual family. Twin-flames are able to pick up on each other's energies in times of crisis or separation. If one half of the soul is upset the other can sense this. They can contact each other through dreams. Twin-flames met before earth and agreed to grow in their lifetimes together. They witness such things as 11:11 and other double-digit numbers on clocks, computer screens, license plates or billboards or even some sort of numerology that represents the other soul, such as anniversaries, birthdays, or death dates. They have unconditional love for one another.

Even with hardships Twin-flame love remains. To be able to meet your Twin-flame is truly a gift from God. With separation and hard times with your Twin-flame unconditional love will remain because you and your twin soul are one. Twin-flames usually have circumstances that will lead a way back to each other during separation. If one soul has found another person to share their life with after meeting their Twin-flame, the relationship is not likely to be as powerful or spiritual as the one they had with their Twin-flame. Love making between Twin-flames is usually very intense. If there are hard times with your Twin-flame it is because on a spiritual level the two souls allowed it for growth. The test of Twin-flames is through unconditional love. If one soul is hurting the other will too. One soul must be strong to show the other how to be strong. With this comes healing inside one soul and spiritual growth. Because of Twin-flames unconditional love for one another they will most likely remain together. Twin-flames always seem to return to one another. If one soul leaves the physical plane, most likely within time, that soul will return to its Twin-flame. For the connection to one another is on a spiritual level. It is a blessing to meet your Twin-flame.

Twin-flames feel so much longing and connection to each other. Twin-flames have the same core Soul frequency. The harmonic tone of this exact vibration creates a magnetic pull towards each other through the universal

Etheric Vibrational Energies. The Divine plan is to sense and feel the opposite half of your soul. This offers a potential for soul expansion and unconditional self Love and acceptance, which is why we are here on Earth, to journey into unconditional Divine Love. With Twin-flame love, there is an intensity that may be overwhelming at times when dealing with your exact mirror.

On January 22, 2008, my life changed forever! It was a Tuesday evening; I was home with my children and boyfriend, Jon. They were watching the news about a 28-year-old actor found dead in his apartment. Suddenly, I felt compelled to walk over to the television and watch the story. When I saw a photo of the actor, I was drawn to him immediately, but did not recognize him. I asked my children what was his name, they told me, but still I could not recall the name. I couldn't move from the television. I was mesmerized by the whole story. I felt very attracted to him, loved his accent and was curious about his life and death. Why was I feeling like this? I could not understand my intense attraction to him. Throughout my life, many young actors have died, but none have affected me the way this man has. It was almost as if I knew him, but didn't know where or how. I had a sudden feeling of connection and love for him. I had no idea what this meant but I was glued to the news. Afterwards, I had to watch some of his movies. I knew there was something to this but had no idea what it was. I started on a journey of finding out all about his life and death.

Compelled to watch one of his movies, that evening we all watched the first movie he made in America. Throughout the movie, I sat smiling as if I knew him. It was amazing how I felt, but why was I feeling this way. I had a strong connection to him, but didn't know why. Later, I decided to look him up on the Internet to find as much as I could about him. I needed to know all about his relationships, whom he dated, his career and why he died so young. My heartbeat would speed up whenever I look at his photos. What was going on? What is wrong with me? Why did I have these intense feelings for this actor? I felt it was more than just a schoolgirl crush; I was too old for crushes. I was feeling deeply in love with a man, I had never met. At least, that's what I believed.

I was in a 13 yearlong relationship at the time but I ended it shortly after finding out who this actor was to me. It felt absolutely right that I had to end this relationship, and within a few months I did.

For months after that, I couldn't stop thinking about this actor and the connection grew to strong feelings of love. I felt bad he had passed so young and I felt like I was going through a loss like you would for a family member. I would be at work, thinking about him and I would be at home, thinking about him. This was starting to worry me a little. Was all of this just a delusion? Then I started feeling that maybe he was very spiritual as I was and that was the connection we had. Maybe we thought alike. But the connection kept getting stronger and stronger. I wanted to be with him so badly.

We are alike in many ways, our mannerisms, the things we like, the way we are with people, our love of humanity and animals, our laugh and somewhat in our looks.

I feel that we have a spiritual mission to bring unconditional love to the Earth. To tell our story and inform others that Twin-flames do exist and come together to show what true love really is.

I was married two times and divorced both. I was never truly in love or happy in either marriage. I was always searching for something, for that special love that I never had. I felt very lonely and disconnected in life and always felt something very special was missing from my life.

My parents were very strict. I was never able to do the same that other children my age were able to do. My family also was very loving but very strict. I have two brothers and one sister. I am the oldest of four children. I lost my youngest brother at the age of 41 in 2003.

I was raised Catholic but never really followed it as an adult. I am very spiritual now.

I was having dreams of this handsome mystery man a lot and when I would wake up I wanted so much to find out who he was and where he was. I was so in love that it drove me crazy. I wanted to be with him so much. The feelings were so intense for him and his for me.

I have never loved like I love Heath ever before. I feel very complete even with him in spirit. I have not dated since I found out about Heath being with me in spirit.

I never knew what a Twin-flame was before all this happened to me. I only knew of soul mates. This is the most amazing, loving and beautiful experience I have ever encountered. I love Heath with all my heart and soul. I can feel him always. He never leaves me; he does whatever I am doing. I can feel him touching me, kissing me, holding me, playing with my hair, and there is also lovemaking, which is incredible. Better than any human I have ever been with. The love is totally intense.

Chapter Seven

Dawn and David

I'm Dawn and my Twin-flame (still not used
to that term) is my husband Dave.
He and I met almost five years ago and just
had our 4th wedding anniversary.
He's thirteen years older than me and seems
to have been 'trained well' by his previous
four wives - haha.

It's funny that his past marriages are what
brought on our discussion about getting
married. I was telling him about my last
serious relationship and how I used that
man's past four wives as my excuse for
rejecting his proposal, telling him I wasn't
going to be anybody's number five.

Dave said, "so that means I shouldn't ask?"
(I hadn't known THAT much about his past,
just that he had been married before)
Needless to say, I changed my mind about
being a number five.

We have the oddest things in common.
My first name is the same as his Mother's.
His middle name is the same as my Father's.

He's the youngest of five boys in his family.
I'm the youngest of five girls.
Lots of silly stuff like that.

Also, goatees have a bad association for me
and I wouldn't have given him a second
glance if he'd had one. Turns out he had
shaved his off just hours before we met :)
It's our differences that seem to be what
makes us so perfect for each other though.
I am extreme in all emotions and many
actions, while he is the picture of
moderation. He keeps me grounded. I take
him on my flights of fancy.

I was married once before and widowed at
twenty-five. For eleven years, I dated several
different men, but knew none of them were
just right.

I knew I'd never "settle" and had gotten past
the point of being content with my life the
way it was. I was happy and the idea of being
without a partner didn't bother me at all. I
guess I got good at being single.

Wouldn't you know it? Life doesn't seem to
like it when we get too comfortable with
something and that's when we get thrown a
curve-ball.

So, I happened to be off work early one day and stopped at the little club in my town on my way home. There was a man I didn't know and could tell he was definitely out of place. I knew if I didn't meet him then I'd never see him again in my life. He said that he decided to stop in on his way back from job-hunting in the larger town past mine. I thought, "that figures. Nobody but shiftless guys hang out in places like this anyway." I figured he must just be another good-looking guy that might be fun, but I couldn't shake the feeling that there was something special about him other than the physical stuff I thought was clouding my judgment.

There was. I found out later that week when we agreed to meet at a little restaurant that he wasn't job hunting because he was out of work. He'd simply taken a day off for an interview with a better company.

I was impressed with the fact that he called me the next night after we met. He said he knew it was common to wait a week or two, but he didn't like playing games like that. Neither do I.

Anyway, we were married eight months later and I keep waiting for the other shoe to drop. It just doesn't seem fair for me to have this much happiness. But I definitely intend to keep appreciating every day we have together. I know from the past that life is short.

(I usually watch him drive down the street every morning before I can make myself shut the door. I don't want to miss out on a single second of him.) I do know how lucky I am and I have no intention of taking it for granted.

So, that's our story.

Chapter Eight

Rachel and Nikola

I think of a Twin-soul as a soul that is split in two, to live multiple incarnations at once for advance spiritual growth. Since they are living two lives at the same time, when they return, they have memories of two different life experiences.
They are one and the same soul...

My childhood was really tough. My mother was neglectful and her husband was extremely abusive. I usually kept to myself and always found ways to entertain my mind. When I was with my father he said that I'd be so quiet that he was always worried something happened to me, but just found me quietly talking to myself in my room. I was born in Texas and grew up in the countryside of the Ozarks of Arkansas and Missouri. I enjoyed the rolling hills and the beautiful natural scenery there; I have an older sister and three younger half brothers. My father took us in when I was eleven and things got a lot better.

I never could figure out what my spiritual beliefs were when I was younger. I never agreed with any church I went to, and spent a lot of my life lost and confused. I later started reading different spiritual and new age books, even books on shamanism, which I found fascinating. I suppose my spiritual beliefs were just being a spiritualist, basing my beliefs on my own experiences and that of others. My connection with God grew stronger over time once I learned to love myself and to connect with others. To me, God is love and our source that we are all a part of.

I feel that I have a spiritual mission which may have something to do with hypnosis. I have had many dreams of studying hypnosis and starting a spiritual group who researches different spiritual phenomenon.

Relationships have always been lousy for me; I was never good with them. I was always too clingy, jealous and picky at the same time, becoming disillusioned when the men in my life didn't turn out to be what I expected. I never could trust anyone and I fell in love very quickly. I even had someone ask me just why I loved him. I was dumbfounded that he would even ask me that.

When I first started channelling, an alien

showed up to communicate while I was taking a shower. I was frightened, but he wanted to tell me that I have been attracting men that reminded me of him. I was confused and refused to channel any more after that, because I had a fear of aliens. But he was persistent and showed up in a dream shortly after that where he took my hand and we floated into a city. We floated past water and onto a pier. I looked around and felt very happy, and knew that I had lived there. It felt very much like home. Then we flew off down through the city where he told me again, "You are attracted to men who remind you of me." I laughed and said, "I'm not attracted to aliens?!" He told me that he was before in a human body, "We were both humans in that lifetime, and we knew each other."

I then understood what he was talking about and he took me back to my bed where I laid back down. He shrunk down to my height (because he was taller than me) and entered into my body. I immediately woke up and felt very strange. I felt like I had no emotions whatsoever and was completely mellow. Of course I got upset because I didn't know whom this alien was and didn't like not having my emotions because I felt that they defined me. I was afraid that I had become possessed. But then I realized something, the night before I had written a letter to Nikola Tesla because I had come to watch a Youtube video on him and was curious. Since I was also practicing channelling I gave him permission to enter my body. I said, "Please, come to me in a dream and talk with me for a little bit, I'm curious to know more about you, I also give you permission to enter my body." I then proceeded to burn the letter so that it would get to him faster. When I suddenly remember what I did, I thought to myself, could Tesla possibly be the alien in my dream who entered my body?

That same morning, I walked into the living room and my sister said out of the blue to me, "Oh, do you know that Tesla thought he was an alien?" I was shocked that this was coming from her. She then said that she knew I was watching some videos on the subject and just wanted to share what she knew.

Curious about the city in my dream, I went to the Internet and did some searches on pictures of cities. I saw a picture that fit the image I saw in my dream and clicked on it and it lead me straight to a website dedicated to Nikola Tesla of all things. It was the first picture I clicked on too. It was Manhattan, where Tesla lived and died in a hotel room.

It was then that I realized the connection. The men in my life were tall and lean, and I was incredibly attracted to intelligence. I have a portfolio of drawings that I have made of cartoon character mad scientists that I've seen on TV. I also found that all of those cartoon characters were based off the same man, Nikola Tesla. No wonder, I thought, I've been chasing after him my whole life. My relationships were doomed from the start because I expected them to be like Tesla, and they weren't.

I even had a dream shortly after I told my friend at work who was related to Mark Twain that I was related to Whistler, where I was being chased by a giant raven while Edgar Allan Poe was reading his poem, "The Raven." I was frightened and then realized that it was silly to be afraid of a large bird and turned around to face it. When I did, I saw a painting of Whistler's mother, though it was Tesla who was sitting in the chair. The picture started to change and he stood up and started walked towards me. I was then told, "The chase is over."

I'm not as picky or controlling as I used to be after having realized this. I'm more open and accepting as to whom I let into my life. I think he saw my struggle and wanted to help by bringing this understanding into my life.

I always felt that there was one man out there for me. I knew my entire life that he was out there somewhere, but deep in my soul I knew that he wasn't alive. I remember looking up at the sky at night and asking, "Where are you, my scientist? I know you've passed on, but I can't find you, not even in my science books." I later discovered why I couldn't find him. He had been practically omitted out of our school textbooks, even after he had contributed so much to our society.

But I have also realized that there are other Soul-mates out there that I can have long and wonderful relationships with as well. I feel that he will always be there for me, but more in a spiritual manner.

The dreams started a few years ago after watching a cartoon of all things. There was one character that I was unusually attracted too, a mad scientist and ghost. He seemed to be the embodiment of everything that I was looking for in a man – well in cartoon form anyway. I remember one dream where I was standing in the forest next to a stream. He materialized and was all misty and white. He looked around and then smiled. He was happy with where I brought him. I smiled and reached out for him. He then reached out for me and faded away. In later dreams I would discover more and more about him. He loved nature, the mountains, caves and waterfalls. He has told me that our love for Mother Nature brings us closer together, or something like that. His character in my dreams didn't fit his cartoon character persona exactly and it was a bit confusing.

In one dream I asked him if we were Twin-flames and what did Twin-flame mean anyway? He didn't have an answer at that time, but later on he showed up in yet another dream where we were in Arkansas (he seemed to like that state that I lived in for a few years) we were in bed and I put my hand on his chest. He smiled and I felt an incredible love emanating from him. He turned to me, looked right at me and said, "We are the same soul." I felt the love again, a strong connection as if our souls were mingling and connecting. It was at this point that I realized that he was a real person not just a dream or a figment of my imagination. He then told me that I was his soft soul and that he loved my softness. I'm not sure what that meant though.

Later on when he would show up, he seemed to drop clues. He showed me a hotel room, and picture of an x-ray, a waterfall, a bird, riding on a dark brown horse in the hills, a cave. When I started to read his biography, I was astonished with the consistencies. In one particular dream he showed up as a cartoon, we were talking and he had a necklace on with a cross. I looked at him and said, "I didn't know you were a Christian." His clothes then changed into a gray suit, and he suddenly didn't want to show me his face. He told me that he was Catholic. Later on I found that his father was an Orthodox Christian priest and the strange suite he was wearing in my dream in time revealed itself in some pictures of him that I came across.

I only told my Dad about this recently. I was afraid that he would think that I had lost my marbles and was just making it all up. But he was actually open about it, especially when I told him about all of things that I've experienced. He was amazed of how everything fit together. Other than that, I haven't really told anyone else in my family.

I confided with a friend at work about it. She and I seemed to really click right off the bat and she was also having strange spiritual things happening to her in her dreams that she couldn't explain. She too was struggling with some issues about not being able to have children so I loaned her some books about past lives and hypnotic regression. They seemed to have the answers that she was looking for. She has told me several times that she felt like we were meant to meet each other. Later she told me that she was related to Samuel Clements, or Mark Twain after I told her that I was related to James Whistler. Shortly after this when I was reading up on Tesla, I discovered that Samuel Clements was a close friend of Tesla's when he moved to America and that reading his books helped him through a period of time when he was extremely sick. Tesla told Clements that his books saved his life and the two really bonded.

When I first realized who was showing up in my dreams, we had already had a relationship. It just felt like continuation of a relationship that we've had for a long time.

I was engaged and have had relationships ever since things have started with Nikola. It doesn't seem to bother him. I've only known about him for about a year now, but he's been showing up for more than a couple of years now in my dreams.

As far as personality goes, he is more calm and collected. I am more emotional and expressive. He's very thin, where I've always had weight problems. Although when he first started to enter my dreams, I had somehow found the motivation to lose sixty pounds and have kept it off ever since. He has no hair; four fingers that taper down, a large head and large eyes with big pupils. I also have unusually large pupils and have always disliked hair. Both of us share that dislike.

We both have the same favorite numbers, three, six and nine. I remember a time where I was dreaming about him and I woke up suddenly at 3:33 pm while taking a nap. I looked at the clock and I could still hear him and he was saying, "Look at the time!" And seemed very excited about it. At the time I wasn't sure why he was excited about it until later on when I found that it was his favorite number and would only do something or eat things in numbers of three. We both have had OCD at some point in our lives, although I must say that his used to be a lot worse than mine. We both love birds, animals and nature and believe that mankind should strive more to work in harmony with Mother Nature instead of trying to control her. We have both felt that we didn't belong as humans on Earth. He confided to close friends about this and I used to pull my fingernails off when I was only three and asked my sister why I had them (he doesn't have fingernails). We both went to a polytechnic university. We both have had careers in technology.

I think I bring in an element of creative

expression and openness to different experiences. He brings a stabilizing calmness and wisdom.

It is certainly nothing like any other relationships I've had in my life. I can't experience the incredible love and connection with other people like I can with him because loving him is like loving myself. I have had other dreams of merging with others and they were just wonderful and incredible. It was all about knowing someone on levels you would never think possible before. Being one with someone is greatest form of love I have ever experienced. It has changed my life.

I remember taking a nap one day, dreaming that I felt his presence and then a golden light started to permeate throughout my body. I felt an incredible amount of love. It was like a love within myself yet it felt like it was from him too. I didn't see him in that dream, I only felt him.

If you want to find your Twin-flame, just ask to meet them. Write a letter to your guide or to God asking to meet your Twin-flame. It may take a while to get the answer, but when you do, the wait will be worth it, believe me. I don't feel that everyone has one in their current lifetime, and some like me don't even have them in this dimension, but you can still meet them in dreams and share many wonderful experiences together.

Tesla has a habit of showing me the future. In one dream we were standing next to a cliff overlooking a city with all these blue lights. I couldn't see much but he was himself. I started to feel uncomfortable and said, "you're dead." So he transformed before my eyes into an alien and I felt more comfortable. I felt softness around me and he called me his soft soul again. I smiled and asked him if we were in the future, and then woke up.

In another dream I was a tall man with dark hair working as a maintainable man in a building. I was working on something in the ceiling, I think it was the air conditioning and I was living in Arkansas. I didn't make a lot of money, lived in a small house and hardly had any furniture. I had a girlfriend with long dark hair, and I loved her because she loved me for who I was and didn't really care that I didn't have an extravagant place to live in. Shortly after that dream I had another where I was in the woman's body and he was my boyfriend. He struggled to pay his bills and ended up losing his house. I had to ask my family for money to buy it back in a bank auction. We later ended up buying a restaurant, but I'm not sure how we managed to do that.

I wondered about these dreams from time to time, pondering why I dreamt about being in both bodies. A couple months later I had another where we were back in Arkansas, and he morphed into himself as we were in bed talking, though at that time, he didn't show me his face. That was the dream where his clothes changed into a suit and he had a necklace of a cross. I looked at him and said, "I knew it was you!" I was excited and happy about it, but at the time I didn't know about Tesla.

Shortly after I discovered who Tesla was, he would show up again, as himself, but for some reason when he was older, getting up on a chair in a building and working on something in the ceiling as if he was fixing the air conditioning ducts. I was there wondering just what on earth Tesla was doing. This dream happened twice until I realized that they were connected to the Arkansas dreams where he morphed into himself to prove to me that it was he. I often wondered if he left something in the air conditioning duct where he lived and was trying to show me that.

It was like a giant puzzle to put together. I was given all the pieces and had to put them all together. He likes to send me messages from time to time such as, "My love extends to you beyond all bounds." and it always lifts my spirit because I feel a strong surge in my heart as it fills with love.

He has make efforts here and there to prove things too me. One time I was wondering if he really loved me or not and even asked that before I went to bed one night. The next day I suddenly felt an urge to get some Chinese food as I was driving home from work. As I sat in the restaurant I felt as if he was there with me and felt incredible, with love all around me. I chuckled to myself because a funny thought came to my mind about a house or something, I can't remember what it was exactly, but it felt like it was almost as if he were saying it to cheer me up. When I got my food and got home, I felt like there was something I needed to know from the cookie. I broke open the fortune cookie and it read, "This person's love is just and true, you may rely on it." It felt like it was the answer I was looking for and it made me really happy.

Chapter Nine

Yin-Yang*

We met at a Mind Body Spirit Show. As it happens we live five blocks from each other. He is fifteen years older than I. He is 52 and I am 38. I knew the second I met him his energy was like a fingerprint imprinted on my soul.

We started a friendship immediately cause we were both married it was well after a year before it became physical. He was in an eighteen-year marriage and I was in a twelve-year marriage.

My marriage fell apart very quickly. I met him in April 2007 and separated from my husband in Jan 2008, He is still physically in the house, with his family, but ended his relationship in May 2008. We both tried marriage counseling but it didn't really work. He is in the process of selling his house and actually moving out. We have been together for two years.

We are very much alike in that we see things in people that other people can't see. I guess we see the Authentic Self of others, also we know that this world we live in is all an illusion. Usually we are not adjusting to the physical we more relate on the spiritual and emotional levels. We also feel and hear each others thoughts and feelings when we are apart. One of the major things that we experienced was when we would look into each others eyes we could see ourselves, and that was the beginning of healing for us both. We learned and allowed each other to begin to love ourselves first and very intimately. During the early stages of our relationship we developed TRUE intimacy (not physical) and that was an amazing feeling and still is today after all that we have had to go through. In the beginning the chemistry between us was crazy and the pull was so strong to be together...we both had a hard time with really understanding what that was, but in time and patience we realized that we were each others other half. With the healing that has transpired in both of us we feel complete within ourselves now and that is a huge gift.

We make each other look at our stuff that comes up for healing and don't allow the other to ignore it. Our lives are always in the NOW when we are together and love each other on such a deep soul level. We respect each other and our own individual journeys to just stand by each other not fixing or taking on each others shit.

We know that the energy between us is so strong that it creates a third entity, and people are affected by us when we are together but they can't figure it out. We feel that we are channels to raise the consciousness of others so they can tap into their Authentic Selves and start to heal.

Before I met my Twin, I was always searching for something never felt complete or whole; I am in recovery now as well and have been sober for almost two years.

I basically grew up by myself I was living on my own when I was 15 years old. My family life was dysfunctional, total broken home, tons of half brothers and sisters almost ten in total. There were affairs, sexual abuse, psychiatric wards, rape, gang rape, physical, abuse, drugs and alcohol. Basically anything to get out of myself and to shut down and self medicate.

I didn't believe in Religion, even though people tried to get me to conform to it, it never felt right and didn't resonate with me. I just always felt energy and identified with energy on all levels.

My mission seems to have started about four years before meeting my Twin Flame. I was dead inside and just existing it was so painful. I went through the dark night of the soul right before I met him and it continued about six months after meeting him.

I have never had a healthy relationship I'm just blown away by how things have transpired with this new relationship; neither of us were looking for this at all.

I never felt there was one person out there for me, but that one energy that could relate and accept me for exactly who I am. I wished for it many many times, but never knew that I was manifesting it way back when.

I don't have physical memories of past lives together but I do have energetic memories in my soul of past lives with my Twin. In the present we have such a connection and psychic things that happen, such as he hears my thoughts and I travel at night to him in Astral and he knows I am there.

I am not aware of any karma between us, but I do know we have unfinished past stuff. We have been doing a lot of work on healing individually and together. As for karma with previous relationships I'm not sure. But when my marriage ended I knew that the soul contract was done and I needed to be free and on my own to heal up so to speak.

This is the most unconditional loving relationship I think any person could experience and for what every reason we have been blessed to be able to experience this. It is mind blowing at times to get your head around the intensity of it, mostly when you are with someone physically the feelings of chemistry wax and wane but we have never experienced this yet...every time we are together sexually it gets more intense and more deeper levels of love. Everything is different...total acceptance would be the biggest thing for both of us; we don't have to even try it just flows without any effort.

I didn't look for my Twin I just manifested him but didn't know that was what I was doing at the time.

If you are looking for your Twin-flame the best advice I would give is to heal up within first and really go deep, let your Authentic Self come through and you'll get in touch with that pureness that has never been touched.

I strongly believe that in order to really experience the deep bond with your Twin-flame you must do the work first within yourself and be complete on your own. If you allow yourself to heal up and really do the work the benefits of knowing that your other half is right there and accepts you for exactly who you are at this moment is priceless. The other thing that I am experiencing with my relationship is a lesson that it is not really helpful to have expectations with yourself and others, you need to be in acceptance of the other even though your mind is telling you that you should have something more or better. The biggest gift we give each other is to experience the NOW and that feeling is magical, it is like there is no time and to be that present to someone is intense.

UPDATE

I am still very much involved with my Twin-flame and he is in the process of cleaning up and ending a 20-year relationship. He needs the time and space to do this, so I know in my soul that we will be together but not necessarily on MY time, it is coming soon and I thank my Guides for all the lessons and gifts that have been revealed with this very special bond with another.

Remember one thing the Law of Attraction will manifest your Twin Flame when it is the right time for you to handle this gift.

*Names changed by request

Chapter Ten

Lisa and Christopher

Chris and I met in 2003 when I decided to join a dating website. We were immediately attracted to each other's photos and both paid the joining fee just so we could send a message to each other. We both said it was an overwhelming attraction, especially as it was only online. After talking online for a month we met in person. We dated for six months before deciding to move in together and lived for six years together and then got married. We have had a few bumps a long the way, but have been happily married for four years now and haven't looked back.

When we met, we lived one village apart, in the United Kingdom. I am from the USA originally and we had come to the realization that I had certain life events occur to be in this country so we could meet.

Christopher was separated from his wife before we met and I was casually dating another man. Christopher proceeded with his divorce and I ended the relationship with the other man straight away.

We share the same spiritual beliefs and

abhor religion. We both share the same outlook on life and what's important to each other. Christopher can be more cynical and flippant and I can be more serious and motivated. I look at things more from a spiritual point of view, whilst Christopher looks at things from an earthly point of view.

Christopher is very good at keeping me grounded and in the here and now and I am good at motivating Christopher and keeping his outlook positive and showing him a different way of seeing things. We feel I am meant to help Christopher awaken to remember why he is here.

Lisa-

I had been married before and immigrated to the UK from America. I had been a single parent for four years before I met Christopher and my whole life was just about my daughter and making her life happy.

Whilst I came from a single parent family, I had a very happy childhood with love and help from both parents; I lived in a beautiful place growing up and was very lucky. We played outside and it was a safe environment, I had a lot of close friends and went to good schools.

My parents divorced when I was five, but I had a loving relationship with both and they got along with each other. I have one full brother. My dad remarried when I was eight and I gained a step mom and a stepsister who I love dearly. We all laugh and have fun when we are together and we are a very close-knit family.

Growing up I attended either a Baptist or Calvary church, which never resonated at all with me. I then became disillusioned and considered myself Agnostic with an, I didn't know and I didn't care attitude. It wasn't until 2005 when I lost a close family member and had a visitation from them and my spirit guide did I start my spiritual journey.

I grew up always feeling different from the rest, very restless, not sure of my purpose here and never felt I fit in anywhere, only with a few select friends. I have always been drawn to helping people, even putting them before myself. I have never known which direction to take this in, but job wise, I have taught and work as a nurse. It's only since the last three years that I have understood my mission as a healer and light bringer.

Relationships were always good in the beginning, but found as time would go on, my spiritual and emotional needs were not being met. I always felt something was missing and never felt I could be myself. I always knew there was someone out there for me; I knew it as I always felt like a puzzle with some missing pieces. I was young I would dream of a darker haired man who I was very in love with. I never saw his face in my dreams, but usually when I woke up I would cry because I was not with him and the dream was always so wonderful. Since I met Christopher he is the one in my dreams if I dream of a man, love etc. I have dreams of past lives with people who are not in my life this time. I haven't been able to recognize their souls as such.

At that time in my life, I was dating casually and not quite sure of what Twin-flames actually were. I had not awakened yet. I went by my intuition upon meeting Chris and my feelings from that.

If you want to meet your Twin-flame, I would say you really need to be at one and loving yourself and this will make it easier for if you do meet them. Just because they are your twin flame, it doesn't mean that the earthly relationship will be easy, in fact you may have many challenges to overcome, but it will be worth it in the end.

Chris-

Before I met Lisa I had a typical work five days a week, come home, have tea. I seemed to have spent too much of my previous relationship not trusting my ex-wife.

My family life as a child was on the whole very good. I was protected from most things. I was closer to my dad, less so with mum. I have two older sisters

In relationships there were mostly with mistrusting previous partners. I was probably too immature at the time. I always felt that there was that one person out there. I'm more aware of karma now through life experiences

This relationship with Lisa is much better, more equal. I don't have the anxieties about my current relationships I used too. Finding Lisa was like Potluck, I got very lucky.

When looking for your Twin-flame, take your time. Never rush into a relationship. Trust and use your intuition. Share common beliefs, whatever they are.

Things are so much easier once you find your twin & there's little reason to argue once you find that person.

Chapter Eleven

Shonna and Bill

About two years before I left my ex-husband I started getting a strange flash of a vision. In the vision I was with a man, whose face was not visible, and my two girls. Sometimes I was pushing a stroller. It was cool outside. We were walking down the street and it was around Halloween according to the decorations on the houses. This vision would come in a flash. As soon as it came, it was gone. What was more intense than the vision was the emotion it gave me. I felt intense love, acceptance, safety, and most of all happiness. I was convinced that this was a sign that I should continue working very hard on my very rocky marriage.

My marriage had not been good pretty much from the beginning. At this point I had been with my husband for ten years. We had two daughters together, both unplanned. The first daughter came after only knowing him for a year. That's right, I became pregnant with her only months after meeting him. It wasn't a fairytale situation to say the least. I always tried to make the best of it believing

that this man was the father of my children
and I owed my family at least that much.

As time went on, he began to drink more
and more. I tried to ignore it but it was
difficult to do. After the vision, I worked very
hard on my own happiness. I decided that I
was going to be happy in this marriage no
matter what. After all, we are all in charge of
our own happiness. I knew that if I wanted to
be happy I had to be happy. Period. I either
had to accept my life how it was and make
the best out of it or leave him and start over.
I wasn't ready to leave. I had two young girls
and was a stay at home Mom. Looking back
I realize it was more about me feeling stuck
than trying to work things out. I was afraid to
leave. Still, I forged on like a good wife and
loved my husband, as I should. Things went
pretty well for a few months. Then one day I
woke up in the middle of the night. I had
trained myself to do this. I would wake up
around 3 or 4 in the morning to go check the
computer. He would pass out after drinking
all night and leave the computer on. It wasn't
uncommon for me to find porn left up. I was
always afraid of my girls waking before me
and finding it. This made me furious but all I
could do is wake up, check, and turn it off.
This particular night I didn't find porn. I
found his email. I know I shouldn't read

other people's emails but I did. I read it. This email was from a woman. She talked about how much she enjoyed talking to him online and on the phone. How she always had a crush on him in school (they attended high school together) but was too afraid to say anything. She said that she never loved her husband the way she loved him. She also said some more graphic things that I will not go into right now. I stood there reading this email and I felt like a ton of bricks had fallen on me. I printed it out and went back to bed.

I can't remember how long it took me to confront him about this. Maybe I did it the next day or I waited a day or two. I don't know. When I did confront him, he faced it the same way he did every confrontation. He blamed me. First he said it was my fault for not having sex with him enough, and then he said I nagged him too often about drinking, and then he turned it around by saying I was crazy and didn't know what I was talking about. This was pretty much the routine. I knew it well. I knew that any confrontation would lead to me feeling like I was crazy and making it all up. That's why I printed the email. I had proof I wasn't making it up. This went on for a couple of weeks. I was faced with her contacting me and being pretty rude as well as him not owning up to what he had done. I found that there had not been any physical betrayal. But it did still feel pretty awful to have another woman have a mental/emotional affair with your husband and fall in love with him. Especially when he defended it all.

A few months went on and I pretended to be ok. He promised to stop talking to this woman and I agreed that would be best. I never felt the same as I did a few months before. I figured I could still be happy though. I didn't need him to make me happy. I could do it on my own.

One night in August, a few days after my birthday he and I got in a horrific argument. We had never argued like this before though we had argued pretty bad prior to this. We argued for hours, probably a good four hours. It started over his disapproval of my friends. He saw that I was trying to better myself. I was learning how to have a life outside of him and he didn't like it. Of course that's not what he told me but I knew that's what he was saying. I defended myself the entire time. I tried to stay calm but eventually lost it. We screamed. I cried. We said nasty things to each other. I was totally drained. Around 3 am I decided I had enough and I went to bed. I lay there in my bed in a state of exhaustion. I was too tired to fall asleep but almost comatose and couldn't move. Several minutes later he crawled into bed with me. I tried to pretend I was asleep because I had no energy to fight anymore. Before I knew it he was on top of me trying to have sex with me. I tried to push him off. I told him to get off. I said no. I cried. I fought as much as I could. I was weak. I had no more fight in me that night. I couldn't do much about what was happening. I was too drained. Finally I gave up fighting. I lay there and cried as he did what he had to do. When he was done I screamed at him to get out of my room. I got up, locked the door and cried myself to sleep.

The next morning was Sunday. I pulled myself together after a horrible night and only a few hours of sleep. I got my girls up and went to the only place I knew to go. I had been meeting some friends on Sundays for our spiritual group. It wasn't church per se though it was like that. We would get together for an uplifting, positive message and feel better for doing it. I told a few people what had happened the night before. It was difficult for me to say but I really needed support at that time. My friends were amazing. Several of them gave me the option of moving in with them or other things that I could do. I decided not to move out, not yet.

The next few months were just a blur. I went about the motions pretending to be married but in my heart the relationship ended that night he raped me. The Monday after the incident I began looking for a job. I looked for two weeks with no luck. I was beginning to lose hope. One day while visiting my daughter's school I saw there was an opening in the cafeteria. I applied. It took a few weeks for them to run fingerprinting, get the paperwork together, and drug tests, etc but I got the job. I was so happy to be working and knew it was a way for me to get out of the marriage.

In January I told him I was leaving. He begged me to stay. I couldn't. I didn't love him anymore. When I looked at him I saw someone totally different. It's amazing how someone can look different to you like that. One day I saw him one way and the next, a different person. He was ugly, disgusting really. I didn't like looking at him at all.

It took me four months to finally get out. I couldn't find a place to live that I could afford. My Mom convinced me to move in with her. Although I didn't feel like it was a good idea, I did it just so I could get away from my husband. I didn't like her boyfriend that lived with her. He treated her very badly. I tried to stay out of it. All I could do is try to make my Mom see that she deserved better. One day it backfired.

Two weeks after moving in, I received a call at work from her. She told me that they had been in a fight and the cops came. They took him away and she wanted me to come. I took off of work and went to support her. The following week it was apparent that she went to see him where he was staying. One night she came home and told me that he wanted to come back. She said he wouldn't come back if I was there. He told her that it was he or I. She chose him. She gave me until the next day to get my things, my girls, and move. I was at a loss. I had no idea where to go. I was heartbroken. I had to move back in with my husband.

I moved into the house I tried so hard to get away from. I was living in a haze. I felt as if I was watching a movie. I was numb. During this same time, the man I had been seeing turned out to be a total con artist, literally. I found out he had lied to me about everything including his name. This just added to my humiliation and depression. I became suicidal. I didn't think I could live with the pain I had any longer.

My best friend of 17 years must have picked up on this. We have always had a tie with each other. We are spiritually connected in some way. She called me and called again, and again. I wouldn't pick up. She left messages for me screaming to call her back. She knew what I was thinking. I did call her eventually. She talked me out of killing myself. Telling me that I had to be there for my girls. She was right. They were the only things keeping me here. They were the only things I wanted to live for.

With her help I found an apartment and moved out of my husband's house within a week. It was a small apartment, only one bedroom. I didn't care. I just wanted to get out so I did. It felt amazing.

Over the next few months the visions of this happy time began to appear more and more. They lasted for longer periods of time. Then began to be accompanied with visions of the back of the man's head. I still was not able to see his face but it gave me hope that I would once again be part of a family.

I was ok with being alone. I didn't need a man to take care of me. For the first time in my life I was happy just for me. It was wonderful. I still missed having a family though. I love being in a family. I knew that I had a family even then. It was my girls and I.

There were days where I was very unhappy and days where I was on top of the world. Still receiving these images and feelings more and more. At one point they would happen several times a day. I longed for those visions. They made me feel so wonderful inside. I convinced myself that they were just my minds way of making me feel I could get through this rough time in my life. Deep down though I knew they were more.

Eventually I started feeling a presence of a man that was in as much pain as I was. I could see the man and he was the same as the man in my vision. He was hurting, sad, and lonely. I would try to tell him to find me and that it would all be ok. I felt like I was crazy but I did it anyway.

Eventually I met a man online who was going through a divorce. He had been separated from his wife about as long as I was separated from my husband. As we got to know each other, our feelings grew more and more. His divorce became final a month after mine. He came to see me about six months later.

When he did, we hugged and I felt his energy, his loving spirit. It was then that I realized he was this vision. He felt exactly like I had felt all of these times when I got this flash in my mind. He had found me we found each other! After coming to this realization it all made perfect sense to me, his sadness, loneliness. It was all around the same time he was having problems with his wife.

I don't know where those visions and feelings came from. Still to this day I know it sounds crazy and overly dramatic. Almost like it should be some stupid girly movie, but I can't deny what I felt and saw. I can't deny that this man, the man I am with now, is the man from my dreams and visions. Because of him I was able to carry through so many difficult times in my life. His spirit came to me without his knowledge over two years before we ever met. I can't explain this but it happened. Whatever it was, I am thankful for it. I am thankful that he and I found each other. I am thankful that all of those rough times are behind me and that I'm a stronger person because of them.

We began chatting on Myspace. Bill is thirteen years older than me. We were 1700 miles apart when we met, we were both going through a divorce, and we were both separated from our former spouses.

I knew we had a connection when we met face to face the first time. After three months of meeting each other we became fairly serious. It kind of just evolved over time. The longer we knew each other, the more serious we became. Now we have been together for about three and a half years, and are married.

Both of us are independent and strong willed. We have similar views when it comes to the important things like raising kids, money, and marriage. Politically we have different views. He tends to be more conservative while I'm more liberal. He is more of a laid back person while I'm more high strung. We tend to even each other out. Whereas he is more likely to be kind of solitary, I'm more likely to be outgoing. I bring him out of his shell some, while he reels me in and keeps me grounded.

I believe that we met when we did so that we can finish the work that we came here to do. He gives me the security to do the things I need to do without worrying about the details like making money or those types of things. I can focus more on my need to help others heal and spreading light to those in need.

Looking back I had a fairly good childhood. I grew up in a strict Christian home. My parents did the best they could but they did not allow for much spiritual growth, only religious. I have no memory of my parents loving each other the way that I imagine two people should. They were distant and cold to each other. However they did put on appearances to be happy. When I was 17, they divorced. My Dad always had a difficult time showing affection to both my Mom and I. I had no siblings. I was an only child. My Mom relied on me to be her support and love. I felt burdened by it sometimes. She was not able to do anything on her own, and always needed me to go everywhere with her. She is to this day incredibly low in self-esteem and continues to choose poor relationships. My father became an alcoholic after leaving my Mom but he is now in recovery. He later remarried and had another son who is the same age as my oldest daughter. He still struggles with his demons.

I grew up Christian. I went to a very strict church that preached to us that we were the only people in the world who were going to go to heaven. Everyone else was "lost". It eventually became a sort of cult. There was talk of moving to a compound but that never came to be. I was always thought to be the bad seed because I was constantly asking questions. These were usually questions that they could not answer. I left the church when

I was seventeen.

I feel I am here to heal and help others. I have not yet worked out exactly how that is going to happen but I know I came here for a special purpose. I remember being asked to come back. Though I didn't want to, I agreed I would.

I never had a good or strong relationship until I met Bill. They always left me feeling empty. From an early age I knew there was someone special for me. I felt a strong sense that I had to find him. I felt depressed and sad because I couldn't seem to find him. I just knew there was supposed to be more in a relationship than what my parents had or what I had been experiencing. I don't remember a time when I didn't feel that way. I remember, as a teenager, using that as my birthday wish ever year...I would wish I would find that special person for me.

Bill and I often have the same idea at the same time. For example, if we are talking either he or I will say something. Then the other person will say, "That's what I was thinking". This happens almost every time we are brainstorming about something. I can also usually tell when he is upset about something at work. I don't sense any karma between us.

I had karma with my ex-husband. I

remember a past life with him where he felt he had wronged me. I was given the message that he had the chance to right the wrong in this life.

This relationship feels much more secure and healthy. We communicate so much better. We work things out, or really try hard to do so. Although we do have our fights and problems, we make a real commitment to make things better. We seem to both be working at it where before I always felt like I was the only one. I also feel like I know him completely. Sometimes he will start to tell me a story about his life and I feel so surprised that it was something I don't know. A feeling I feel like I just know all about him but then realize that I really don't. I suppose that feeling is more of a soul level knowing where when it comes to human level I don't know him as well.

To find my Twin-flame I used lots of prayer and spiritually talking to him to find me. We did eventually meet online.

I believe that others first have to work on themselves. They need to really find those lessons that have to be learned. Forgive the people who may be holding them back from spiritual and personal growth. Become whole. Do not expect another person to fill your voids or make you happy. Although you do not have to be perfect, you should at least honestly understand that you are the only person who in charge of your own feelings and destiny. Putting too much responsibility on another person for those things in your life can be too much of a strain on the relationship. I believe that it's ok to use another person for support but we must be confident enough in ourselves to stand-alone too.

I would like to mention that although it is incredible to find your flame, do not believe that it does not still require work. Like any relationship, there is ongoing work to be done. We cannot think that because they are our Twin-flame we can just set the relationship aside. Make your relationship a priority in your life. Love that person and commit to them to do what needs to be done to make it a healthy relationship. If you are both willing to do this, it can be a relationship that can stand the test of time.

Bill-

I knew after the first trip to see Shonna that we had a special connection. Before we met I was going through a second divorce. I had lived alone for most of my adult life. I went to work and came home. I never really got out to meet people.

I had a good childhood; I was well cared for

and enjoyed my life. My father and grandfather raised me. I had one half brother and one sister.

I believe in a great being but am not religious. I have always felt a desire to protect others.

All of my relationships before Shonna were always empty, wondering why the other person never offered more of herself. I hoped there was that one person for me but was beginning to think I would never find her. I feel more comfortable and at ease with Shonna, it feels right. Shonna actually shows me that she cares about me, not just what I can do for her.

My advice in looking for your Twin-flame, is don't try too hard. Don't over analyze. Relax, enjoy the ride and keep an open mind. It will happen when you are both ready. Things are never easy in any relationship. There will be times when you will disagree but as long as you communicate things will work out.

Poetry

I Remember...

In the beginning

You & I were ONE

One flame divided as TWIN

To eventually reunite

And meld again!

I remember

Our first assignment very vividly

The power of our love

Propelled and guided Galaxies

Across all of time & space

As God and Goddess of a Celestial Race!

Assignment #2

Would physically separate me from you.

You remained in the UPPER ROOM

I volunteered to go

As it is above so it is below.

Guiding me from Heaven with unconditional love

As I transform in the Earth plane to the purity of a dove.- Author unknown

You crossed my path,
When I least expected you.
Through time travels,
We have always been together.
A love so strong and deep,
The expanse is unfathomable:
When you crossed my path,
The Heavens sang with utter joy,
And Mother Earth,
like a child in wild ecstasy,
Danced to the rhythm of love's revelations.
An eternal love that was complete
Through our vows to God and us.
Beams of light shone through the clouds
As the crimson sky rejoiced.
The tides licked at our feet,
As though anxious for a taste of love.
The wind teased us with gentle blessings
and caressed our hearts with pleasure.
And as the eternal song was being played
And celebrated with glorious enthusiasm,
Our hearts beat together as one,
Like a gale of laughter resounding in our
hearts

Author unknown

———

Just a Dream

Through the dawning of the morning
I watch the iridescent window
let the warm and gentle sun stream through
and
I marvel at the splendor I awoke to gaze
upon

I must release my thoughts of evening and
search for a tomorrow, for a place that may
spread some peace upon my soul.

I wonder as I lie here, how our paths just
seemed to cross, with no unspoken memory
of how we chose to be a part.

Just a brief and gentle dream, where our
lives enmeshed in joy.

I wonder, if somehow, we chose to see a sign,

of a life beyond our normal and
somehow connected on a plane above.

In a dream, perhaps you held me, as you did
once long ago, and called out to me gently
as I turned my head to go.

Was there someone else beside me in my

slumber, or a dream just invented in my head?

You seemed so real and I can still remember your wooden shack and soft dirt floor....

© Katrina Bowlin-MacKenzie

Passions Dream

In the night beyond myself dreaming,

Sensing a flicker of deepest feeling

A call reaches out from Sister soul to Brother

I am a lion stirred by heart song of another.

Rising from this stillness of tranquil slumber

A lover's calling awakens the hunter

Muscles launch, forbidden senses spy the
prey

A chase begins but myself I cannot slay

I am gazelle darting through brush,

Body surfing air, hooves thundering the rush

Till ground is ablaze, alight with life's
passionate ride

Screaming breath filling chest for one more
stride

Soul blasts into being amidst lightening rings

And I fly, I am the fire upon wings

Soaring to invoke dawn's sky, earthly planes
tremble

Beneath my breadth mountains assemble

Waves gather, rolling across a quaking ocean

Caught in the force of love's emotion

Dark void opens to consume my mind

And stands before the one, the one I must find

A Phoenix explodes into the sun as Venus kisses Mars

Heavens ignite into shards of stars

Ten thousand angels sing of love's plea

as I fall through dimensions into the arms of thee

©Phoenix MacKenzie

_____

Two Souls Intertwined

You are the warmth in my heart
The fluttering in my soul
By myself I am complete,
But with you I am whole.

You are the twinge inside
The ecstasy I've never known
Alone I can find peace,
But with you it's more profound than I've
ever known.

Whether we're together in a year,
In a decade, or the life after this
We have been one from the beginning
Two souls intertwined no one can dismiss.
©Dawn

Twin-Flames

I did not know I was a part
and not a whole.

I only knew I felt a
yearning in my Soul.

Then in the warp of
fate my life touched yours.

In a sudden burst of light
Nova Bright, I understood.

When Love is right, the glow
illuminates the darkest night.

You have made me whole
stopped my wandering, searching for my
Soul.

I did not know that what I longed for
was the rest of me.

The half of me that you held
in your heart.

©Katrina Bowlin-MacKenzie

———

KNOWING

Knowing who holds
The Perfect fit to your soul
Before the time they are meant to be
together
Brings both
Comfort and Profound Love
As well as
Pain and Profound Impatience.

But if we trust in it
And Everything around us
The Divine forces that made us conscious
now
Will bring us Together as One
When our work apart is Done.

©Dawn

___

The Long Path

From the forest was I taken
From love was I torn
To an ocean of loneliness reborn
Smashed upon the rocks of life
To dwell upon unforgiving lands
Party to unfolding mysteries
Great labors wrought by mine hands
Suffering the scorn and doubt of man
Wandering beneath darkened clouds
Offering Light to those lost
Mine own way forsaken to prophets shrouds

Despairing at humanities folly
Through battle fields carrying the rose
Shielding Love from blood and pain
Protecting sanctity from dark shadows
Across lands of war and horror
Caring for those wounded in vain
Compassion in a world of bitter fears
Till dead was I amongst the slain
Temples built in ancient ages, then anew

Still alone wandering through life
Still searching, ever searching for the way
But no soul on the path was mine souls wife

Born to life after life in service
Till even sight became mine night
Whilst Masters spoke of the day and dawn
So painfully tested was the Light
Ravaged by witches of darkened heart
Entangled by those empty within
Search, ever searching for a soul
Longing for the love only she could bring
Yet never to end seemed this test
Mayhaps Great Spirit forgotten such promise
And death the only path to paradise
Mine life again would end to this

Broken, empty without love forsaken
A fallen guardian lies upon the path
Heart ripped from mine chest
Strength relinquishes the falling white staff
Blood mingles with blind tears
The warrior lays dying with last breath a plea

Forgive me Master but thy servant can serve
no more

Without Love there is only a path to
nowhere

Have mercy upon my soul

In death a hand reaches out

To an invisible forest where once he knew
love

Mists of mystery swirl over the fallen devout

Screams of an ancient cry echo through time

This death had she felt before

Long, long ago in her arms

upon lands of another life's shore

Die must such pain, her own life slipped
away

To his own sword she grasped and fell

Fire of a burning soul grasped her hearts
seed

Lifting their love from her empty shell

"Together again shall thee be"

Whispered a memories promise in divine

tongue

"Leave not now love, mine soul shalt honour the promise

And to thee I will come"

Though hope so small, the seed of her love touched

And the guardian cannot rest

Whilst others must learn to know love

Into other hearts understanding manifest

The mist touches all in their separation

And brings such sorrow to the fallen

Abandon them he cannot

Whilst hearing the Love of her calling

And so Light lifts him again to Life

The dead rises to his feet

Walking again the long path in hope

That one day the trinity will be complete

That her Love may know this lonely soul

And kiss a smile upon the face of sorrow

Wandering through the cries of love

Hopping that the face of joy will be his tomorrow

Through it all eternity whispers of such
promise
That all will one day know
Light and Life are empty without Love
To that understanding all will follow
Yet so distant they seem now
So many have so far to go
As I look back upon the world
Mine soul beckons them all to know.

The Path Home
Gazing before him only into darkness
From the mist a path winding through life
Whilst within the forest a silent cry
Her loss stabs as though a sacrificial knife
Each step into mortals world now a cut
Along the path so cold, so old
Walk it again the guardian must
For there is truth yet to unfold
Weight of duty and armor crushing
Blood stained with lives lost for what must be
One more step toward the dawn
when all will awaken free

Last glimpse toward an invisible forest

That's shadows whisper "look away, look away"

Leaving here an empty heart

For hope shall only lead astray

He walks this day toward a tomorrow

Toward a dawn that never rises

Guiding lost souls along forsaken roads

Enduring betrayal in many disguises

Though none may touch the warriors heart

For there is no longer a heart to hold

Their lives would they give to know his soul

But to him love is so cold

Walking with many beyond illusions of need

Only to leave them there like angels to fly

Onward to the edge of their dreams

His own wishes the guardian must deny

Winters of fate call upon the devout again

To bless others with love he must never feel

Heal within sleeping angels the path known well

And bring them to the only thing that is real

Dark shadows of forgotten promises ever taunting

"Look away, look away"

So many seasons of emptiness pass toward death

Till what was dead whispers "come, rest today"

The warrior waits for eternal night to take him

Within the forest where once he knew love

Heart and hope long buried he weeps from soul

Tears of the night born of heavens above

Yet the day will not end whilst phantoms roam

Shimmering faintly beneath leaves and time

A ghostly sword beckons memories wounding deep

To truth the sword sings - a sword once mine

Like all that was lost it vanishes to my grasp

And with it the tears a soldier must not show

To feet, to stand, to beyond here now

I cannot remain where I must not go

Deep in the forest roamed another soul

Weary of unfulfilled passion but one could
gift

This place was hers and hers alone

Alone this priestess through memories did
sift

In an invisible forest where once she knew
love

In many woodland had this priestess dwelt

Though only one was haunted by the ghost

The ghost of a love she once felt

All around gathered beasts of nature

Drawn to beauty and heart enchanted

She the sparkle in a stream, the gem within
stone

Yet there was sorrow in the smile she granted

Time would not take him into the night

He whispers a plea upon bended knee

And turns to a long path that invites to
wander

Beyond this temple of ancient memory

Toward the march of time he walks in vain

Mist obscures the path and way

Such foolish wish for a face he will never see

Far distant a cry near kills his soul "stay my love, stay"

To ground he falls in writhing agony

Stabbing mind with such lie

The wind brings more he dare not hear

And beckons his soul to fly

For a moment time holds his breath

The stream ceases to flow

Clear waters gifting to her a sword

That once she took so long ago

Still waters scatter to her fall

Within her heart beats such pain

To touch what was true once more

But her reach bursts sword into flame

And she cries "stay my love, stay"

Faintly, so faintly to her ears a distant song

Again stream flows with her tears

For she thought the melody of wings gone.

Silent this night as still they lay

Still as death in disbelief

Her eyes became pools of light

Spirit of the earth lifts him from grief

Armor flickers like burning embers

For within burns a heart of elemental fire

His breath calls forth the wind

And thunder summons him higher

A flaming bird spirals to the sky

To sing that she may dance in souls grace

Colors of seven veils fall in a forest

The last that he may see his Wife's face.

So long, so long such beauty unseen

Hidden from any mortals eye

For such radiance would blind

Those that would speak of love with a lie

In an ancient forest where once they knew
love

Two hands reach out toward each others

Great Spirit's promise whispers in the mist

That one dawn they shall again be lovers

Upon ground once stained with blood

Two swords lay side by side

These ghosts shall only rest and be one

When their masters in love abide

The Alchemical Wedding
Walking a razors edge of past and future
Through storms the voice of love calls
To travel, to seek the promise
Of long paths heights and falls
From mountains have we gazed
oceans of time and tide crossed
Searching for one-another and the love
Without which we were lost
And there is no one or anywhere
That knows contentment, to rest, to call home
To be held in such beloved embrace
For without each other we are alone
The forest beats to the heart of all souls
And all paths lead to sorrows ravine
To the bridge of broken hearts
So far into depths do tears fall unseen
Upon the edge of deaths lip two gaze
Across a void to what is beyond sight
And across fate guides their steps

On the bridge to where day meets night

Mist swirls about them like the dance of life

Weaving together what was once undone

This bridge healed in a moment of sublime
love

As two swords and two souls again become
one

And so my love I greet thy beauty

I give my life to thee without fear

So long have I traveled the path to thee

And now my love I am here, I am here

Two halves of one heart united

Listen sweet love for the angels sing

Within our tears they sparkle

To the world heaven shall we bring

So long, so very long the path

Of the dream to you

Some say the stuff of fairy tales

Yet this dream is so very true

I whisper now of secret things

Sacred and silent they are

To a temple were these souls called

So too were many of worlds near and far

From the shadows, from the light

From the fire, from the sea

From the earth, the sky and veils between

Did gather elementals for the fifth to be

Stag, bear, salmon and hawk nature called

Within a circle of blossoms, a temple of tree

And there shall be spoken rites of ancient
lore

To unify soul, element and the trinity

Light and Life now whole in Love

Two mortals blessed with what soul doth feel

Though tis true the path to love knows much
pain

Tis like the tempering of fine steel

From the earth cometh, through fire formed

With water cooled to sing the air

To cut and slay that we need not

To live as we are, if any so dare

Through leafy fern little eyes gaze in wonder

As now two swords sing as one

Many wings rise to open

Under the violet fire of loves new sun.

©Phoenix MacKenzie

Conclusion

Further advice regarding Twin-flames

1. Discernment is very crucial. When one encounter a strong pull of energy towards someone, don't be rushed, but take your time to wait, to listen to your inner divine guidance, to acknowledge what it's about. One needs to discern what type of relationship it is, one needs to discern everything they found on internet, or what they listened to from spirit guides, one needs to be patient, one needs to wait... if the symptoms closely look like Twin-flames it might be a heart center catalyst relationship, when the heart center opens, one may experience a connection with everyone/everything and they could feel everyone/anything is their Twin-flame. They may be experiencing past life memories but not all mean it is a Twin-flame connection. And those spiritual journeys might just be in preparation for getting someone ready for a more meaningful, higher vibrational relationship in the future.

2. Learn about Twin-flame relationship from a credible source, a Twin-flame couple that can provide you with information about the

true-life experiences of being in the relationship. The 'how to's', and the process. Don't bother with information from people, sites or books that say they are experts in Twin-flame relationships but they are not even with their Twin-flames, as that could be fatal.

3. I personally am concerned about mass information about Twin-flames on Internet that are imbalanced and do not cover the whole truth about this type of relationship. This makes people over obsessed with romantic relationships. It is sad to know that many people are living in an illusion; they thought they were with their Twin but actually not. It is sad to know that many could be leaving their marriage for their Twin as they read one or two articles that do not even touch the surface about the true reality of this type of relationship. Twin-flame relationship is not about romance or one's own self-fulfillment, or an ideal type of partnership, it's greater than that. It's about service, it's about a dedicated life, it's about assisting humanity, it's about working, and so romance is just a very small part of it. So, enough of the spiritual entertainment, time for the truth.

Fancy

Born in San Diego, CA and now living between Northern California and South Wales, UK

Katrina is the mother of four wonderful grown children, the grandmother of nine, (seven grandsons and two granddaughters). Plus she is great grandmother to two very precious little girls.

She is an Intuitive, a Healer, a Psychic Counselor and an author.

Her published works include:

The Beginner's Guide to Psychic Development-published 2009
Ancient Echoes, a paranormal/romance/fantasy- published 2010.

Seven children's books-
A Fairy Tale, The Secret,
Bluen Island and Missing Lissa
all published in 2011

Honor's Magical Imagination
Lizzy The Reluctant Princess
Brooke's Magical Adventure
All published in 2013

All the information on her books is available at her Facebook Author site, http://www.facebook.com/KatrinaBowlinMacKenzieauthor

or her website at

http://mystweaver.wix.com/k-bowlin-mackenzie

Katrina can also be contacted at

myst.weaver@yahoo.com

Printed in Great Britain
by Amazon.co.uk, Ltd.,
Marston Gate.